Ashton Oxenden

The Parables of Our Lord

Ashton Oxenden

The Parables of Our Lord

ISBN/EAN: 9783744760034

Printed in Europe, USA, Canada, Australia, Japan

Cover: Foto ©Lupo / pixelio.de

More available books at **www.hansebooks.com**

THE

PARABLES OF OUR LORD.

BY THE

REV. ASHTON OXENDEN,

RECTOR OF PLUCKLEY, KENT.

"NEVER MAN SPAKE LIKE THIS MAN."
JOHN VII. 46.

LONDON:
WILLIAM MACINTOSH,
24, PATERNOSTER-ROW.
1864.

LONDON: WILLIAM MACINTOSH,
24, PATERNOSTER-ROW, E.C.

CONTENTS.

	PAGE
INTRODUCTION	1
THE SOWER	14
THE TARES AND THE WHEAT	30
THE MUSTARD-SEED, AND THE LEAVEN	42
THE HID TREASURE, AND THE PEARL OF GREAT PRICE	55
THE FISHING NET	66
THE UNFORGIVING SERVANT	78
THE LABOURERS IN THE VINEYARD	92
THE TWO SONS	105
THE WICKED HUSBANDMEN	116
THE MARRIAGE SUPPER	127
THE FORGIVEN DEBTOR	140
THE NEIGHBOURLY SAMARITAN	153
THE RICH FOOL	165
THE FRUITLESS FIG-TREE	178
THE HUMBLE GUEST EXALTED	191

LONDON: WILLIAM MACINTOSH,
24, PATERNOSTER-ROW, E.C.

CONTENTS.

	PAGE
THE LOST SHEEP	203
THE PRODIGAL SON. Part 1	214
DITTO. Part 2	228
THE SHEPHERD AND THE SHEEPFOLD	241
THE DISHONEST STEWARD	252
THE RICH MAN AND LAZARUS	263
THE WIDOW AND THE JUDGE	278
THE PHARISEE AND THE PUBLICAN	290
THE TEN VIRGINS. Part 1	302
DITTO. Part 2	314
THE SERVANTS AND THE TALENTS	326

INTRODUCTION.

WHY DID OUR LORD USE PARABLES? AND HOW SHALL WE BEST UNDERSTAND THEM?

A PARABLE is a kind of story, which has in it a hidden meaning—a story which is intended to teach us some spiritual truth.

This was a mode of teaching, which our blessed Lord seemed to take special delight in employing. And we may be quite sure, that as "He knew what was in man" better than we know, He would not have taught by Parables, if He had not felt that this was the kind of teaching best suited to our wants.

O blessed Saviour, do Thou teach us by Thy Holy Spirit, as we read these portions of Thy word; and open to us those precious truths which are able to save our souls.

There are some few Parables in the Bible, besides those which Jesus spoke. In Judges ix., for instance, we find one. We there read of Jotham speaking a Parable to the men of Shechem. He wished to reprove them for having chosen Abimelech as their King, and he thus addresses them :—" The trees went forth on a time to anoint a king over them; and they said unto the olive-tree, Reign thou over us. But the olive-tree said unto them, Should I leave my fatness, wherewith by me they honour God and man, and go to be promoted over the trees? And the trees said to the fig-tree, Come thou, and reign over us. But the fig-tree said unto them, Should I forsake my sweetness, and my good fruit, and go to be promoted over the trees? Then said the trees unto the vine, Come thou, and reign over us. And the vine said unto them, Should I leave my wine, which cheereth God and man, and go to be promoted over the trees? Then said all the trees unto the bramble, Come thou, and reign over us. And the bramble said unto the trees, If in truth ye anoint me king over you, then come and put your trust in my shadow ; and if not, let fire come out of the bramble, and devour the cedars of Lebanon."

Here was a sharp rebuke to Abimelech, and to the people of Shechem who had chosen him for their king.

In 2 Sam. xii., we find the Prophet Nathan also making use of a Parable, in order to convince David of his great sin in having taken away Uriah's wife from him. Nathan knew how very difficult it was to bring home a man's guilt to him. And he therefore thought that if he were to go to him, and at once accuse him of his crime, he would forthwith begin to defend and excuse himself: so he addressed him in the following most touching Parable:—
"There were two men in one city; the one rich, and the other poor. The rich man had exceeding many flocks and herds; but the poor man had nothing, save one little ewe lamb, which he had bought and nourished up: and it grew up together with him, and with his children; it did eat of his own meat, and drank of his own cup, and lay in his bosom, and was unto him as a daughter. And there came a traveller unto the rich man; and he spared to take of his own flock,

and of his own herd, to dress for the wayfaring man that was come unto him; but took the poor man's lamb, and dressed it for the man that was come to him. And David's anger was greatly kindled against the man; and he said to Nathan, As the Lord liveth, the man that hath done this thing shall surely die: and he shall restore the lamb fourfold, because he did this thing, and because he had no pity. And Nathan said to David, Thou art the man."

There are also three or four more Parables in other parts of the Old Testament.

In some of the old Jewish Books too, which were composed long after the Scriptures were written, we meet with actual Parables, written after the same manner as the Parables of the Bible. I will give you one out of many.

The Writer is wishing to show why good people so often die when young. "To what (he says) is this like? It is like a king, who walking in his garden, saw some roses which had as yet only buds, breathing forth an unusual sweetness. He thought, If these shed such sweetness while they are buds, what will they do when they are fully blown?

After a while, the king entered the garden anew, thinking to find the roses now blown, and to delight himself with their fragrance. But arriving at the place, he found them pale and withered, and yielding no smell. He exclaimed with regret, 'Had I gathered them, while yet tender and young, and while they gave forth their sweetness, I might have delighted myself with them, but now I have no pleasure in them.' The next year, the king walked in his garden, and finding rose-buds scattering fragrance, he commanded his servants, saying, 'Gather them, that I may enjoy them before they wither, as they did last year.' " *

Here we are taught by a very beautiful Parable that God sometimes takes away His people early, out of love to their souls, knowing that, young as they are, they are ripe for His presence.

So much for Parables generally. But what we are most concerned about are those in the New Testament, which were spoken by our blessed Lord Himself. These Parables are

* Quoted by Archbishop Trench.

beautifully simple, and yet full of matter. They are "like apples of gold in pictures of silver." They are "fair in their outward form, but yet fairer within."

Now, in the three first Gospels we find several of these Parables. But it is remarkable that St. John gives us only one, namely, that of the Sheepfold, in the tenth chapter.

Next, let us enquire, *Why* our Lord spoke in Parables. Why did He, who was the Great Teacher sent from God, adopt this mode of giving spiritual instruction?

1. Jesus Himself gives us a reason. For on one occasion, when the disciples came and said unto Him, "Why speakest thou unto them (that is, to the multitude) in Parables? He answered and said unto them, It is given unto *you* to know the mysteries of the kingdom of heaven, but unto *them* it is not given: therefore speak I unto them in parables, because they seeing see not, and in hearing hear not, neither do they understand." He meant by this, that He was anxious that those, who really desired to know His truth, and were willing to seek for it, should find it. But He

wished that it should remain hidden, and locked up, from those who did not value it. Oh that we may earnestly seek after, and find, the precious lessons, which these Parables contain!

2. Another reason why our Lord spoke thus was, because anything in the shape of a story interests us more, and makes a livelier impression on our memories, than if the same instruction was given in another shape. A tale or story takes our fancy. When we hear it, we are at once all attention. It stands by us too for years. And this is the reason why there is no portion of God's word that we remember so well, and turn to with such delight, as the Parables which Jesus spake. How very graciously and kindly did our Lord in this way meet our wants, and consider our infirmities!

3. Again, perhaps He spoke thus, in order to show us that we should turn to good account the things which are constantly meeting our eye; and to show us also that we may thus get help in understanding the highest and holiest truths. He teaches us for instance that when we sow a field with corn; or observe

the weeds growing up; or lose one of our sheep; or cast a net into the sea—there is something to be learnt from it. And if only our minds are set on things above, how much there is in the commonest works around us to teach us lessons which may do us good!

4. Another reason why our Lord spoke in parables was, that it was *foretold* that He should so speak. Thus, when Jesus had been delivering a number of these Parables, we are told that He did so, " that it might be fulfilled which was spoken by the Prophet, saying, I will open my mouth in Parables; I will utter things which have been kept secret from the foundation of the world."

These are some of the many reasons why our Saviour spoke, as He did, in Parables; and why they deserve all the attention we can give them.

Let us now enquire how we should set about the examination of them.

First, we should be very careful to *get the right meaning*. We should not be content with *a* meaning; but we should try and gather the *true* one.

Some persons will make a Parable teach what it was never intended to teach. I will give you two or three instances.

The Parable of the Good Samaritan is clearly meant to enforce upon us the duty of *loving our neighbour as ourselves.* This was the object in our Lord's mind. But I have known quite a different explanation to be given. The "Good Samaritan" has been said to mean our blessed Lord Himself; the wounded and half-dead "traveller," Adam and his sinful race; the "oil and wine," pardon and grace; the "two pence," the two sacraments, the Baptism and the Lord's Supper. In short, a meaning has been forced into it quite different to what Jesus intended.

So, in the Parable of the Rich Man and Lazarus, just because the Rich Man entreats Abraham, who was in heaven, to send Lazarus to cool his tongue, some have gone away with the idea that we may offer up prayers to departed Saints. But surely such a doctrine can never be gathered from this Parable.

So again, in that of the Ten Virgins, because five are described as entering into the marriage supper-room, and five as shut out, it has been supposed by some, that out of those who are called Christians, exactly one half will be saved, and half lost.

But surely this again is "making the word of God of none effect." In reading Scripture, we should avoid anything that is merely fanciful; and try to discover the simple, plain meaning, which God would have us gather from His word.

Secondly, when we have one of the Parables before us, and wish to understand it, we should ask ourselves, What is *the general scope or object* which our Lord seems to have had in view? We shall be able to gather this from the context—that is, from what goes before, or follows after. We shall thus see what led our Lord to speak the Parable; and this will often remove some of the difficulties. Sometimes too Jesus tells us, or the Sacred Writer tells us, in so many words, what the main lesson is which He wishes us to learn. And if you can find out this, it will serve as a key to open to you the great and leading truth which the passage contains.

Thus, in the Parable of the Ten Virgins, of which I spoke just now, the closing verse tells us plainly the great duty which our Lord wishes to press home upon us—namely, watchfulness. "Watch therefore, for ye know neither the day nor the hour wherein the Son of man cometh." This, therefore, is a kind of *key-verse* to the Parable.

So, too, in the Parable of the *Pharisee and the Publican*, St. Luke tells us that Jesus "spake this parable to certain which trusted in themselves that they were righteous, and despised others." Then, we may be sure that the main drift of the Parable is to show us the sin and hatefulness of a self-righteous spirit, and the beauty of lowliness.

Thus you see there are many things to lead us to the right meaning. There are fingerposts, as it were, if we will but look for them, which all point in the direction which we are to take.

Thirdly, we shall do well to remember that *we must dig deep* if we would find the precious gold. Oftentimes it does not lie on the surface, and we must take pains to get at it.

Our Lord's advice is, "Search the Scriptures" —not merely read them, but *search* them. And most assuredly those who search diligently and earnestly *will* find the treasures they contain.

Lastly, I greatly wish my Reader to do this :—Read over to yourself beforehand, very carefully and thoughtfully, the Parable which you wish to have explained. Try, first of all, to draw out all the instruction you can from it without any help. Dig into the mine yourself, before you open this or any other book. If you adopt this plan, I am very sure that you will find the explanation all the more interesting and instructive, and you will really profit by it.

Further, *ask God for the teaching of His Holy Spirit*. This is what we all want. It is not enough to understand the meaning of any passage of Scripture. We want to have it written on our hearts. It must come with enlightening power to our souls; or we shall never feel the true preciousness of God's Word. The promise is, "All thy children shall be taught of the Lord." Oh for more of that blessed teaching! Oh for more of the Holy Spirit in our hearts—making us feel that joy, and peace, and comfort, which the Word of God can and will give us, if it is only rightly received! Let *this* be your prayer, "Open Thou my blind eyes, and unlock my closed heart, so that I may behold wondrous things in Thy gospel."

THE SOWER.

Matt. xiii. 1—8.

"The same day went Jesus out of the house, and sat by the sea side. And great multitudes were gathered together unto him, so that he went into a ship, and sat; and the whole multitude stood on the shore. And he spake many things unto them in parables, saying, Behold, a sower went forth to sow; and when he sowed, some seeds fell by the way side, and the fowls came and devoured them up; some fell upon stony places, where they had not much earth: and forthwith they sprung up, because they had no deepness of earth: and when the sun was up, they were scorched: and because they had no root, they withered away. And some fell among thorns; and the thorns sprung up, and choked them: but other fell into good ground, and brought forth fruit, some an hundredfold, some sixtyfold, some thirtyfold."

See also Mark iv. 1—8; Luke viii. 4—8.

This is generally supposed to have been the first Parable which our Lord spoke.

Let us see where Jesus was when He delivered it.

In the country of Galilee there was a large Lake, several miles across; and on this Lake many of our Lord's disciples earned their livelihood as fishermen. Jesus, having probably passed the night at Capernaum, which was by the water's side, went in the morning, and sat by the Lake. Presently great multitudes flock around Him. He desires to seize the favourable moment, and teach them something for their souls' good. To avoid the pressure of the crowd, He gets into one of the boats, and addresses the people from it.

Try and picture to yourself that scene. It is probably in the early spring. The Lake is calm and unruffled, and a number of little ships are dotted about upon its glossy surface. The Saviour is in one of them, which is nearest to the shore. He suddenly stands up, and speaks as never man spake, with a heart full of tenderness and love for those whom He is addressing. Close by, along the bank, is ranged a group of eager listeners.

And what is *the subject* of His address? It seems oftentimes to have been our Lord's custom to take some familiar event, which was passing before His eyes, and make it the groundwork of His instruction. Probably it was so in the present instance. Perhaps that very morning, as He came to the Lake, His eye may have rested on some labourer, who was busily engaged in sowing his field. This at once supplies Him with a fit subject for His teaching, and He forthwith utters this well-known Parable of the Sower. The object of it is to show that there is a right and a wrong way of hearing the Word of God.

Our Lord begins by saying, "A sower went forth to sow. And when he sowed, some fell by *the way side*, and the fowls came, and devoured it up."

We may suppose that the Field here spoken of had a pathway, either through the middle of it, or by the hedge-side, just as we very often see in the present day. Some of the seed falls on this hard, beaten path; and there it lies on the surface. As well might you expect it to spring up, if dropped upon your room floor, as to see it sink in, and grow, upon that trodden path. No; there it remains, till the fowls of the air come, and fly off with it.

Now, then, let us see what explanation our Lord gives of this part of the Parable. Look at verse 18, " Hear ye therefore the parable of the sower. When any one heareth the word of the kingdom, and understandeth it not, then cometh the wicked one, and catcheth away that which was sown in his heart. This is he which received seed by the way side."

The class of hearers here described we may call *Careless Hearers*. And this is no uncommon class. Many go to the house of God without the slightest desire to profit by what they hear. The word spoken has not the least effect upon their hearts. It makes no impression whatever. They allow Satan to snatch it away, as soon as it falls.

This is sad to think of; but it is most true. What! has God sent us a message, and are there any who care not to receive it? Does He tell us of our sins, and of a gracious Saviour who can deliver us from them? Does He speak to us of heaven and hell? And are these things nothing to us — not worth listening to? Alas!—so it is with some. May it not be so with us!

But let us go on with the Parable, and see how other portions of the seed fared. "Some fell upon *stony places*, where they had not much earth; and forthwith they sprang up, because they had no deepness of earth. And when the sun was up, they were scorched; and because they had no root, they withered away."

The "stony places," mentioned here, were probably certain patches in the field, where the soil was very bare. There was just a thin coating of mould, and the rock or stone beneath. Here the seed quickly springs up, and takes root; and all the quicker because there is no depth of soil to bury it. But almost immediately, it dies away. The sun too, which greatly helps it in other parts of the field, scorches and destroys it here.

We have again our Lord's own explanation of the passage, in verses 20, 21 :—" He that received the seed into stony places, the same is he that heareth the word, and anon with joy receiveth it; yet hath he not root in himself, but dureth for a while: for when tribulation or persecution ariseth because of the word, by and by he is offended."

Now, this describes those whom we may call *Shallow and Unstable Hearers.*

There are some in every congregation, who *listen* attentively enough to the word, whilst the Minister declares it. There is no opposition to it—no cold rejection of God's message; but, on the contrary, a willing acceptance of it. The heart welcomes it; and it awakens a joy in the soul. There is some hope, for the moment, that the heart is touched—that some impression is made—that God's converting, life-giving power is felt within. But, alas! it is only the surface of the water that is ruffled. The arrow has only grazed the skin, and then glanced off again. The feelings are only roused for an instant; but the whole inner man remains much as it was before. A serious thought or two comes across the mind; and presently all passes away.

Is it not so with many? Has it ever been so with you? There has, perhaps, been an inward joy, when the Word was spoken. You felt for the moment as if sin was hateful to you, as if Christ was precious, and as if you could give your whole heart to God. Your soul was warmed within you. That was a blessed time; and oh, that it had lasted! But it was not God's own work, and therefore it did not stand. It was not a tree of His gracious planting. It had no root. It withered away, having no support.

From this portion of the Parable we learn that there may be strong feeling in a person. There may be a whispering of the conscience— a starting up as of one awakened out of sleep. All this may take place; and yet there may be no conversion, no saving work of grace within, no deliberate turning of the heart to God, no blessed fruit showing itself in an altered life.

We may learn further that there is a *trying*, *sifting* time with most hearers. Just as the cutting winds, the nipping frost, and the long scorching drought, all serve to try the tender blade of corn, whether it will endure only for *a while*, or whether it is *fairly* and *lastingly* rooted, even so the Christian has his trials too. Difficulties spring up. He once fancied that religion was an easy matter, but he finds that the gate is strait, and the way narrow. Sin must be put away, and the heart weaned from many things which it used to love. And then too there is persecution to be borne. And it is hard to meet that. It is hard to be laughed at, and abused, and despised, for Christ's sake.

Depend upon it, it costs something to be a true Christian. It is not enough that there be the green *blade* of profession: there must be also the *root* of grace. There must be that within us, which will stand the trial, in whatever shape it comes.

Oh that God would give us more real earnestness and fixedness of heart!

The Parable further tells us that some of the seed "fell among *thorns;* and the thorns sprung up, and choked it."

Here was a better prospect of success to the Sower. Here was some depth of soil. The blade made its appearance above ground, and the root laid firm hold below. But along with it sprang up weeds and thorns; and these grew so rank and strong, that they soon overpowered the good seed, and fairly killed it. You see, in the last case *the stones* spoilt *the root:* in this case *the thorns* spoil *the fruit.*

Our Saviour's explanation may be found in ver. 22. It is this—" He that received seed among the thorns is he that heareth the word; and the cares of this world, and the deceitfulness of riches, and (as St. Luke adds) the pleasures of this life, choke the word, and he becometh unfruitful."

This is certainly a more promising Hearer than the last. His heart is really impressed. He is thoroughly aroused. He goes away with new and altered feelings, and honestly resolves to carry them out. He sees the hatefulness of sin, and determines to forsake it. He sees the beauty of holiness, and has a taste of the joys of a religious life. But he has not counted the cost. He does not consider that his poor feeble strength is but perfect weakness. He soon finds that sundry temptations beset his course.

For instance, *the Cares of the world* press hard upon him. Take the case of some poor man or woman, who has perhaps a family to provide for, and who finds it hard to make his little incomings sufficient for his daily necessities. He gets behindhand. This brings cares and anxieties on his mind. He grows careless about his soul; and by degrees all his good resolutions are thrown aside. He drudges on, as if the wants of the body were his only concern. In this way the good seed is very often choked.

Or *Riches* are his temptation. We will take a person whom God has blessed with enough and to spare. He is well to do in the world. He is a thriving man. His business prospers. He is tempted to set his heart on money. It steals away his affections from better things. It becomes the one thing needful with him, the all-important object in life. And presently God is completely thrust out and forgotten. No wonder that our Lord says, "How hardly shall they that have riches enter the kingdom of heaven." No wonder that the young Ruler "went away sorrowful;" for we are told that "he had great possessions." Here is another instance of the seed being choked with the thorns that spring up around it—choked by *riches*.

Once more—The world has *Pleasures* also, suited to tempt and entice the heart. Men love these pleasures, and live for them, though perhaps all the while they feel their thorough emptiness. And thus these pleasures, poor as they are, are constantly dragging the heart downwards. God's Word is heard and believed. There is a power in it, which brings conviction to the conscience. But then the world's demands interfere with it.

Then comes the struggle. And oh what a hard struggle it is! Every now and then the question comes, Shall I give up the world with all its charms, or shall I give up my Saviour? There is a strong desire at times to serve Christ, and yet an unwillingness to leave all and follow Him. Yes, *all;* for all must be given up—at least we must be *ready* to part with everything, even what is most dear to us, *if He should demand it of us.* And do not many stumble at this stumbling-stone, turn back, and go no more with Christ? Here again the good seed is choked and rendered unfruitful—choked by worldly *pleasures.* Now whatever earthly feeling has at this moment possession of our hearts—whether it be the *cares* of the world, or the *riches* of the world, or the *pleasures* of the world—it must be put away, and that speedily, or the salvation of our soul is imperilled. Do not mistake me. It is possible to occupy ourselves with the ordinary callings and duties of this world, and yet all the while to be doing God's work, and that faithfully. We may be rich too, and yet not set our heart on riches; our treasure may be in heaven. Let us only take care that no earthly thing is allowed to engross and fill our minds, or it will be quite sure to thrust out better things, and destroy the work of grace.

Once more, the Parable tells us that other seed "fell upon *good ground*, and brought forth fruit, some an hundredfold, some sixtyfold, and some thirtyfold."

Here we have the *earnest, believing, decided Hearer*. This part of the Parable speaks so plainly, that there is no mistaking it. Still our Lord condescends to give us an explanation of it in ver. 23—"He that received seed (He says) into the good ground is he that heareth the word, and understandeth it; which also beareth fruit, and bringeth forth, some an hundredfold, some sixty, some thirty."

There is one thing specially to be observed in this Parable. It is that *three unprofitable* kinds of Hearing are described, and *only one who hears with any saving effect.* Some of the good seed falls by the *wayside*, some on *stony ground*, some again drops among *thorns*. This sadly reminds us that on a large portion of mankind God's Word is thrown away. Their hearts are not in a state to receive it, and be blest by it. Few only bring forth fruit unto life eternal.

Let me now put a few things before you, which this Parable clearly teaches.

1st. It teaches that *our hearts must be prepared by God* to receive the good seed of His truth. Do you not prepare *the Field*, before the Sower comes to scatter the grain over it? What if you should only run the plough through it here and there, and leave patches of it hard and unbroken? Could you expect an even crop? Certainly not. Then, why act differently with your own heart? Ask God to make your hard heart soft, to remove your blindness, your impenitence, your unbelief. The next time you sit down to read your Bible at home, or go to Church, kneel down beforehand for a minute or two, and entreat Him to prepare your heart, and to enable you to receive with meekness His engrafted Word. Do this, and you will soon find the blessed effects of it.

2dly. We may learn that in order to hear a sermon profitably, *something more is needed than mere attention*. A person may sit and listen very quietly; and yet carry nothing away with him. I will go even further, and say, a person may remember every word of a sermon, so as to be able to talk about it; and yet he may be but a " wayside " hearer after all. The ears may have been open, and yet the heart closed. The sinner may remain a sinner still. The understanding may be fed, but the heart empty. We may be able to *talk* about a sermon, and yet feel no desire to *act* upon it.

O God, speak to my heart—that is what I want. Speak Thou Thyself to my inner conscience. Shoot Thou the arrow; and may it pierce and wound my soul!

3dly. *Beware of becoming hardened.* Sometimes we see young men and women—aye and old people too—with very hard hearts. Nothing seems to move them. They have no feeling. Their consciences are numbed and callous. What a fearful state to be in! Better any state than this! Better to be alarmed, and anxious, and even miserable, than to be, as St. Paul says, *"past feeling!"*

Remember, *Sin* hardens the heart. *Worldliness* hardens it. And even *the gospel itself* hardens it, when it is often heard, but not heeded. This is the worst hardness of all— when any one is "ever hearing," and yet "never comes to the knowledge of the truth."

4thly. We are reminded in this Parable that there is an *Evil Spirit* ever hovering about us. "Then cometh *the wicked one,"* says our Lord. And *where* does he come? Everywhere he comes; and especially wherever the good seed is being sown, wherever the Word of God is preached. He enters the very house of God. He is one of the first who comes, and one of the last who goes. When any word, that suits the state of a sinner, falls from the mouth of the Preacher, then comes the wicked one, eager to catch it away. When we pray in our secret chamber, he is sure to be there, trying to dart into our minds the most trifling thoughts. When we read our Bibles, he tries to draw off our attention, and to darken the light of God's truth, as it glimmers upon our souls. When we are upon our knees in God's house, he is by our side, and whispers to us about the world, and even about sin. And especially when the great message of salvation is proclaimed, he steels our hearts against it, and uses all the means he can to make it fall powerless on our ears.

Be on the watch then. There is in the Gospel a precious treasure. Seize hold of it while it is offered to you, and make it yours. Take care that no one snatches it from you.

May the Lord, who spoke this Parable of the Sower, make it a warning and a blessing to our souls!

THE TARES AND THE WHEAT.

MATT. XIII. 24—30.

"Another parable put he forth unto them, saying, The kingdom of heaven is likened unto a man which sowed good seed in his field; but while men slept, his enemy came and sowed tares among the wheat, and went his way. But when the blade was sprung up, and brought forth fruit, then appeared the tares also. So the servants of the householder came and said unto him, Sir, didst thou not sow good seed in thy field? from whence then hath it tares? He said unto them, An enemy hath done this. The servants said unto him, Wilt thou then that we go and gather them up? But he said, Nay; lest, while ye gather up the tares, ye root up also the wheat with them. Let both grow together until the harvest: and in the time of harvest I will say to the reapers, Gather ye together first the tares, and bind them in bundles to burn them: but gather the wheat into my barn."

THIS Parable was spoken by our Lord immediately after the Parable of the Sower, and seems at first sight to be somewhat like it. But if we examine it, we shall find it to be altogether different. We have the Field again, as before, and Seed sown in it. But we shall see that the lesson which it teaches is entirely a new one.

A person is here represented as sowing good seed in his field. In the night some malicious enemy comes, and scatters tares all over the ground. The Tares mentioned here are not like our tares; but a kind of grass which very much resembled wheat, though utterly worthless. He is not *seen* doing this: he does it secretly at night, while his neighbour is asleep. The Farmer sees his crop springing up, and has no suspicion whatever that there are Tares mixed with the Wheat. But when it begins to form into ear, then he discovers the mixture.

His Labourers on the farm express their surprise,—" Sir, didst thou not sow good seed in thy field? From whence then hath it tares?" He at once guesses what has happened—he has an unfriendly neighbour, and it must be *his* work. The servants then propose to go, and gather up all the tares they can find. But the Master objects to their doing this—" Nay," he says, " lest, while ye gather up the tares, ye root up also the wheat with them. Let both grow together till harvest-time; and then we will separate them."

And now for the explanation. Here we have no difficulty; for in this Parable, as well as in that of the Sower, our Lord gives His own explanation. It appears that when the multitude were gone, Jesus went into a private house; and there the disciples followed Him, begging Him to tell them the meaning of what He had been saying—"Declare unto us the Parable of the tares of the field."

But before we come to the explanation, there is one expression at the opening of the Parable, which may be misunderstood. Jesus says, " The kingdom of heaven is likened unto a man which sowed good seed in his field." Now, what did He mean by "*the kingdom of heaven*"? He certainly could not have meant Heaven itself; for there are no tares there, no evil ones there. It means the gospel kingdom—the Church of God—Christ's kingdom in the world—that kingdom which Daniel spoke of many hundred years before, when he said, "I saw in the night visions: and behold, one like the Son of Man came with the clouds of heaven. And there was given him dominion, and glory, and a kingdom. His dominion is an everlasting dominion which shall not pass away, and his kingdom that which shall not be destroyed." It is well to bear this in mind; for the expression "the kingdom of heaven" is very often used in the Gospels, and especially in the Parables. Remember then that it means *the gospel kingdom.*

Now then let us see what our Lord would have us understand by this interesting Parable.

"The Field," He says, "is the World"—this world in which we are now living. "The good seed are the children of the kingdom"—holy persons, who truly love and serve the Lord, whom the Saviour now reckons among His people, and who will share His glory hereafter. They are brought into His kingdom by the power of His grace. They are His plants—His chosen ones—the wheat which He Himself has sown and cherished.

But to go on—If "the good seed" are "the children of the kingdom," what are "the Tares"? They, says our Lord, are "the children of the wicked one"—false professors, mock disciples. Satan is their Master and their Father. Though mixed among the wheat, they belong to him. "The Enemy that sowed them is the Devil." He is the great Enemy of Christ; and uses every effort to mar His work, and to destroy His kingdom.

"The Harvest," here spoken of, "is the end of the world;" and "the Reapers are the Angels," whom God will then employ to gather together His elect. "As therefore the tares are gathered, and burned in the fire; so shall it be in the end of this world. The Son of man shall send forth his angels; and they shall gather out of his kingdom all things that offend, and them which do iniquity. And shall cast them into a furnace of fire; there shall be weeping, and gnashing of teeth. Then shall the righteous shine forth as the sun in the kingdom of their Father."

The drift of the Parable then is this—It represents to us the present and future state of the Gospel Church, or kingdom; Christ's care of it; the Devil's enmity against it; the mixture of good and bad in it, of false and true; and the separation between them at the end of the world.

Having thus endeavoured to make clear to you the Parable itself, let us now dwell on some of the different points in it.

First, we learn here that in Christ's kingdom on earth—that is, in His Church—there is, and always has been, a mixture of bad with the good, of false with the true. Just as in a field there will always be a mixed crop; take what pains you may, there will be weeds and blighted ears among the corn; so it is in every Christian Body. There were unclean animals in the ark, as well as clean. There are goats feeding in the same pasture with the sheep. There is chaff on the same barn-floor as the grain. And so here there are Tares mingled with the Wheat.

I say it always has been so. There were Tares in the *Jewish* Church. There were Prophets, "who wore a rough garment to deceive." There were Jewish Priests and Rulers, who put on a mere cloak of godliness.

There were certain members of the Church of God, who were unsound members. "They are not all Israel," says the Apostle, "who are of Israel; neither because they are the seed of Abraham, are they all children."

In the early Christian Church too there were Ananias and Sapphira, and other false Brethren, who "crept in unawares." And even among the very Apostles, the close companions of our Lord, there was Judas the Traitor. Not that Jesus was deceived in him. He could not be deceived. Indeed St. John tells us (ch. vi. 64) that "Jesus knew from the beginning who they were that believed not, and who should betray him."

Sometimes we are ready to ask, How can this be? Can that be a true Church, in which there are false members? Where is that "glorious church," which St. Paul speaks of, "not having spot or wrinkle, or any such thing, but holy and without blemish"?

Here, in this Parable, we have the truest answer. The Church will be pure one day, but not now. The Tares will be gathered out, but not yet. Jesus foresaw exactly how it would be. He sowed good seed; but He knew that tares would come up with the wheat. He prepared us to expect it.

Surely then, when we are disposed to complain that there are many things around us which are not as they ought to be, we should check ourselves. I go to church, for instance; and the man or woman next to me may not be, according to my judgment, a true Christian. I approach the holy Table, and I see among my fellow-communicants some whose piety I doubt. What then? Am I to be disturbed at this? Ought I to make it a stumblingstone? Certainly not. I should rather feel that such *must* be the state of things, as long as we are on earth. There will be this mixture. I must wait for purity and perfection, till I join the Church above. And meanwhile my chief aim should be—ah, this should be the matter which concerns me—that *I* may not, by any unwatchfulness of my own, bring a blot on my Christian profession.

Secondly, we gather from this Parable that one of the great objects of Satan is to sow Tares among the Wheat. His grand aim is to spoil the work of Christ.

Does he see brethren living at unity together? He sows the seed of discord among them. He breaks up their unity, and causes divisions.

Or, does he know that the work of grace is prospering in a man's soul? He is sure to have some crafty device to check it; and if we are not on our guard, he will do so.

Or again, if he sees in any particular place that men are more alive than common on the subject of religion, he will scatter false doctrine among them, or lead them into false practice. And he does this to deceive men, and to bring dishonour upon religion.

Be not surprised then, if even among the people of God Satan sows his Tares. Let us be prepared for it, and say, "An enemy hath done this."

Thirdly, we may observe that men, in their folly, often try to separate the precious from the vile. There are some eager ones in every Church—some who are a little puffed up with a feeling of their own goodness—who are ready to cry out with the Servants in the Parable, "Wilt thou that we go and gather up the Tares?"

Thank God, we are not called upon to do this; not that the Tares shall never be plucked up, but that this is not the time, and we are not the doers. Thank God, we are not sent to judge the world, but to spread the knowledge of salvation in it. What are we, that we should try to set our mark here and there on the people of God? If we attempt it, we shall perhaps make most grievous blunders. Perhaps we shall thrust out many a humble believer; and perhaps we shall let in many a hypocrite. And there is another thing too—Shall we not be in danger of rooting up some who now appear to be Tares, but who may one day, through God's converting grace, be changed into precious wheat? Oh, what wisdom is there in those words, "Judge nothing before the time;" "Let both grow together *till the harvest.*"

And this leads me to speak, *lastly*, of that time when *the Separation will take place*—the time of the world's great harvest.

Look at Rev. xiv., and see what St. John says, "I looked, and behold a white cloud, and upon the cloud one sat like unto the Son of man, having on his head a golden crown, and in his hand a sharp sickle. And another angel came out of the temple, crying with a loud voice to him that sat on the cloud, Thrust in thy sickle and reap: for the time is come for thee to reap; for the harvest of the earth is ripe. And the angel thrust in his sickle into the earth, and gathered the vine of the earth, and cast it into the winepress of the wrath of God."

Here is the gathering out of the wicked from God's kingdom—the rooting up of the Tares—just what the Lord describes in the Parable before us. "The Son of man," He says, "shall send forth his angels, and they shall gather out of his kingdom all things that offend, and them that do iniquity."

Christ will then have a pure Church. Every ungodly one will be cast out; every hypocrite; every one whose heart is false, though his words may be fair. His "people shall be all righteous."

It is well then not to concern ourselves so much about the condition of others, as about our own. Let us see that *we ourselves* are right with God. Let us see that our hearts beat true to Christ. Then shall we be found among " the Church of the firstborn which are written in heaven "—among those "righteous" ones, who shall " shine forth as the sun in the kingdom of their Father."

THE MUSTARD-SEED AND THE LEAVEN.

MATT. XIII. 31—33.

"Another parable put he forth unto them, saying, The kingdom of heaven is like to a grain of mustard seed, which a man took, and sowed in his field: which indeed is the least of all seeds; but when it is grown, it is the greatest among herbs, and becometh a tree, so that the birds of the air come and lodge in the branches thereof.

"Another parable spake he unto them; The kingdom of heaven is like unto leaven, which a woman took, and hid in three measures of meal, till the whole was leavened."

(See also Mark iv. 30—32; Luke xiii. 18—21.)

HERE are two Parables which are so much alike, that we will examine them together.

The main object of them both is to show that God's kingdom is a *growing* kingdom—very small and feeble in its beginning, but gradually increasing, until it becomes great and important.

This is shown by two comparisons.

In the First Parable, God's kingdom is compared to *a Mustard Tree.* Now, we have no such tree in this country; but it is found in hot climates. The seed is very small and insignificant; but after a while it grows to a considerable size; so that it is able to give shelter to the birds of the air, who "come and lodge in the branches thereof."

This comparison of a Tree is not an unusual one in the Old Testament. The Prophet Daniel thus describes the greatness of Nebuchadnezzar's kingdom:—"I saw (in a vision), and behold a tree in the midst of the earth, and the height thereof was great. The tree grew, and was strong, and the height thereof reached unto heaven. The beasts of the field had shadow under it, and the fowls of the heaven dwelt in the boughs thereof." Ezekiel also likens the kingdom of Assyria to a spreading tree—"Behold, the Assyrian was a cedar in Lebanon, with fair branches. His height was exalted above all the trees of the field. All the fowls of heaven made their nests in his boughs."

But our Lord, when He is speaking here of

His own kingdom, compares it to a *Mustard Tree*. Why is this? Many nobler plants, as the vine; or taller trees, as the fir; or larger trees, as the oak; might have been named. But *the Mustard Tree* is chosen for this reason—because the seed of it is extremely small, and yet it grows to a great size. He wishes to show us, not merely that His kingdom will be glorious; but that it will be glorious, *in spite of its weak and despised beginning*.

Then, in the Second Parable, God's kingdom is compared to the working of the Leaven in a loaf of bread. The quantity of leaven that is put into it is very small; but the meal soon swells out into a considerable bulk.

Now, we may apply these two comparisons to the working of God's grace, both in the heart, and also in the world.

1. You will observe that the Mustard-seed is *brought to the field*. It does not grow there naturally. It must be sown. So too with the Leaven. It is *placed in the meal*. It is not naturally found there.

There is something to be learnt from this.

If we are to become really religious, God's grace must come into our hearts. It is not there naturally. It must be placed there by God Himself.

Suppose you wish your field to become fruitful—you may take great pains to improve the soil—you may manure it, plough it, harrow it, and weed it most carefully. Still it will not produce corn, unless the seed is actually brought and dropped into the ground. So you may improve a person's character— you may reform him a little—and yet he may not be a really religious man after all. What he needs is, a new heart, and a new nature— something which he has not got, which man cannot give him: it must come from God. He must be "born from above."

St. Paul says, "It is God that worketh in you, both to will and to do, of his own good pleasure." You see, the *will* is from God—the first feeble desire—the first moving of the heart towards Him—the first inclination to leave the path of sin and carelessness, and to find a better path. Then, too, *the power* to *do* what is right is also from Him. By nature we are utterly powerless. We have no strength of our own. It must be given to us.

Our Church speaks very plainly on this point, in the Tenth Article. These are the words:—" The condition of man after the fall of Adam is such, that he cannot turn and prepare himself, by his own natural strength and good works, to faith and calling upon God. Wherefore we have no power to do good works, pleasing and acceptable to God, without the grace of God in Christ preventing us, that we may have a good will, and working with us when we have that good will."

This is very important, and therefore I dwell upon it. There is a heavenly gift, which we all need; and without it we are utterly helpless and unprofitable. God, who commanded the light to shine out of darkness, must first shine into our hearts, before we can see anything as we ought to see. God, who at the first breathed into man's nostrils the breath of life, must breathe into our souls the breath of a new and spiritual life. He must begin the work, and carry it on, within us.

How is it that one person is religious, and another careless? Is it knowledge that makes the difference? No, there may be much knowledge, and yet no religion. Is it that one has greater opportunities than another? No, those who have the greatest advantages are sometimes the least benefited by them. Is it that one is *born good*, and the other *born bad?* No, we are all of us born of the same corrupt stock, and with the same evil nature. It is that God's grace is welcomed to one heart, and not to another; just as the mustard-seed is received into the ground, or the leaven into the meal. Grace alone makes a person a true believer, a real child of God. "By grace are ye saved, through faith; and that not of yourselves; *it is the gift of God.*"

Oh, then, apply for it. Seek it as a gift from above. Say, "Lord, give me that grace, which can turn my darkness into light, which can make me a new creature, which can fit me for thy service, and fill me with love, and joy, and peace."

2. But now, observe another thing. We see, from these two Parables, *how* the grace of God works. It works gradually, silently, and effectually.

It works *gradually*. What has been the history of Christianity? When Jesus stood by the Sea of Galilee, and persuaded Andrew, and Peter, and Philip, and Nathanael, to join Him, what a poor, despised company it was! Who would have thought that that could be the beginning of a kingdom, which would never be moved? Who would have thought that those few fishermen, who left their nets, to follow Christ, would have turned the world upside down by the truths which they uttered? But here was *the little grain of mustard-seed:* here was *the little handful of leaven*. And soon it grew and spread, till hundreds and thousands owned its power; and it will spread, till "the kingdoms of this world" shall become "the kingdoms of our God, and of his Christ."

And how is it in individual hearts? When a work of grace is begun in any one of us, how small are its beginnings! A single word, a stray sentence, a passing thought, an ordinary action, may prove to be the little seed, which afterwards fills the whole heart. The soul is aroused. The conscience is touched. A feeling of thoughtfulness comes over us.

A little light breaks in upon the soul—only a little. There is still much darkness, but not that thick darkness there once was. The work goes on. The faith, which is but as a grain of mustard-seed, so weak and feeble, grows. The little strength increases. The spark of light kindles into a flame.

The Christian may take encouragement from this. The work of grace is a gradual work: it is not done all at once. God's blessing comes by degrees. A little is given to-day; and a little more to-morrow. Be not cast down, if some have more knowledge of the things of God than you have, more strength to resist temptation, more boldness to confess Christ. Go to the Fountain, and you will receive. "He giveth more grace." "Ask, and it shall be given you."

Next, I would observe that God's grace works *silently*, as well as gradually. It is so with the growth of the Mustard-seed, and so again with the Leaven. There is no sound to be heard in either case—nothing to draw attention to what is going on. And just as silently does God carry on His blessed work, whether in the heart of a private Christian, or in the Church at large.

Some Pharisees once asked our Lord when the Kingdom of God should come. And He answered them and said, "The kingdom of God cometh not with observation: neither shall they say, Lo here! or Lo there! for behold, the kingdom of God is within you."

Some think there must needs be a great stir and noise, when a soul is converted to God—that the change must be *seen* by all. But does Holy Scripture lead us to look for this? Do the Parables before us hint at it? No, just the reverse. What can be more silent and hidden than the growth of the seed in the ground, or the working of yeast in a lump of flour? I am sure there is a work of grace oftentimes begun in a person's heart, when others know nothing of it; nay, when the person himself is hardly aware that the change is begun. Is it not so in the works of nature? The Dew descends quietly and unobserved. We do not see or hear it falling. The Break of Day steals on silently. There is no thunder-clap to announce it. When the Temple of Solomon was being erected, we read that "there was neither hammer, nor axe, nor any tool of iron heard in the house, while it was in building." Yes, and God's saving work in a soul is a hidden work. The dew of His blessing comes down gently, with its refreshing and renewing power. The dawn of a new life breaks silently upon the soul. The spiritual temple is built up, without any outward signs of what is going on within.

And is it not better, far better, if God is carrying on a work of grace within us, that that work should go on quietly and unnoticed? It is more likely to be a sure work, a real work, a lasting work.

Observe also that grace does its work *effectually* in the soul. The leaven, or yeast, leavens *the whole* lump—*all* the meal with which it is mixed. And where there is true religion in any heart, the *whole inner man* is influenced by it, and *the whole character* undergoes a change. Our thoughts, our desires, our feelings, our words, our life is altered by it. In short, "if any man be in Christ, he is a new creature: old things are passed away; behold, all things are become new."

But the grace of God works *effectually* in another way. It does not arouse and awaken the heart, and then leave it. It *goes on* working, till the work is completed. We see this both in the Mustard-seed, and in the Leaven. The grain is dropped into the ground; but it is not left there to rot; the blade springs up, and grows, till it comes to perfection. And the Leaven in the meal works on, until every particle of it is leavened.

And God will not leave you, my Christian Brother or Sister. He will perfect that which concerneth you. Have you begun to feel your soul moved by the love of Christ? Are you beginning to take an interest in His word? Do you find a comfort in prayer, which is quite new to you? Ah, men may think, this will all pass away, and come to nought. No, not if it is a real work of grace. The world may come in like a flood, and almost smother your religious feelings. Your hope may be dimmed for a time. Satan may tempt you sorely, and try hard to bring you once more under his power. But, if God is on your side, He can and will carry you through. Look up, and be encouraged. "He who hath begun a good work in you will perform it unto the day of Christ." "No man can pluck you out of His hands."

There are two more points in these Parables to be noticed.

One is that the ground in which the mustard-seed is sown must first be *dug and broken up*, or the plant will not grow. And again, the meal must be first *ground and bruised*, or the leaven will have no effect upon it.

And oh what bruising and breaking do our hard hearts undergo, when grace takes any effect! Why is it that some of us reject God's grace, resist His Holy Spirit, are unmoved by His gracious calls? It is because our hearts are not in a fit state to receive religious impressions. Like a piece of untilled earth, the plant cannot thrive on it; or like a grain of unground wheat, the leaven cannot penetrate it. It has been well said, "The Law grinds the heart, and then the Gospel leavens it."

The other point to be noticed is this—the Mustard-tree is represented in the Parable as *a shelter* for the fowls of the air. This tells us what the Gospel is to us. It is a shelter for man's great need. Are we sick at heart? Here is a remedy. Are we sad? Here is peace. Are we poor? Here are the truest riches. Are we weary of this world? Here is rest.

Have you found it so? Go, like a poor homeless one, to Christ. In Him there is perfect safety. He will shelter you from every storm, and defend you from every danger.

THE HID TREASURE, AND THE PEARL OF GREAT PRICE.

MATT. XIII. 44—46.

"Again the kingdom of heaven is like unto treasure hid in a field : the which, when a man hath found, he hideth; and for joy thereof goeth and selleth all that he hath, and buyeth that field.

"Again, the kingdom of heaven is like unto a merchantman, seeking goodly pearls; who, when he had found one pearl of great price, went and sold all that he had, and bought it."

HERE again, are two Parables, which are so much alike in the lessons which they are intended to teach, that we will consider them together, as we did those of the Mustard-seed and the Leaven. And may the Holy Ghost be our Teacher and Guide, whilst we examine them!

Let us see what are the points in which they are alike, and in what respect they differ.

First, both Parables describe *something of great value* being found.

Secondly, both represent the prize as *something hidden*, and therefore *difficult to be discovered.*

Thirdly, both represent the Finder gladly *parting with all*, in order to possess what he has found.

But the Parables differ in this respect—In the one case the man stumbles upon the treasure without even looking for it: in the other he seeks diligently, and then his search is rewarded. These then are the points which we will notice.

And First, both Parables speak of *something of great value*. In one Parable it is described as " *a Treasure*," and in the other as " *a Pearl of great price.*"

Now, what are we to understand by this thing of great value—this prize—which is here called a Treasure and a Pearl? Perhaps our Lord meant *Himself* by it; or perhaps He meant *Eternal Life*. It matters not which, since, if we possess Christ, we possess eternal life; for " he that hath the Son hath life."

What are the treasures of earth compared

with this? If we could own all the gold mines of California—all the pearls at the bottom of the sea—if we had all the riches of Solomon—what could they do for us? Would they make us happy? Could they ensure to us health, and strength, and length of days? Could they give peace to a restless conscience? And even if they could do all this for us, how long would it be for? For a few years at most; and then we must part with them, and that for ever. We cannot take our money with us. It would only mock us on our death-bed, and be a burden to us in a dying hour. The Wise Man knew this, and therefore he said, "Labour not to be rich." St. Paul knew it too, and gives this advice to Timothy, "Thou, O man of God, flee these things."

What then is there, which is really valuable? What is that treasure, which is more precious than all else? It is the salvation of the soul—eternal life—the possession of Christ.

And now, that we know what is meant by the Treasure and the Pearl, we will pass on to the *Second* point, which is this—Both the

Parables represent this costly prize as *hidden*, and therefore *difficult to be discovered.*

In the First Parable, you observe the Treasure is spoken of as being "hid in a field." This wants a little explanation. It is not usual in these days to find a treasure concealed in a common field; but it was by no means uncommon formerly. Worldly goods and property were not so safe then as they are now. We are told by travellers, that in some countries, even now, it is not unusual for rich men to divide their goods into three parts. One they employ in commerce; one they turn into jewels, which in case of danger they can easily carry away with them; and a third part they bury. If they should happen to die suddenly, the buried treasure would most likely be as good as lost, until some lucky person, whilst tilling the land, might chance to light upon it. Now, in the first of these Parables, a man is described as digging in a field, and discovering one of these hid treasures.

In the Second Parable too, the pearls spoken of are *hidden* things. They are usually found at the very bottom of the sea; and they are considered so valuable, that persons are specially employed to dive for them at the risk of their lives.

And are not heavenly things entirely hidden from some of us? We can see no beauty and no glory in them. "The god of this world hath blinded the eyes of them which believe not, lest the light of the glorious gospel of Christ should shine unto them." The gospel is spoken of as a "mystery which hath been hid from ages and from generations, but now is made manifest to the saints." And St. Paul declares that "the natural man receiveth not the things of the Spirit of God, for they are foolishness unto him; neither can he know them, for they are spiritually discerned." And again he says, "If our gospel be hid, it is *hid* to them that are lost."

How sad, that there should be salvation for us all; and yet that so many of us should pass it by, like a man who is working in a field where there lies a treasure just below the surface, but he cannot see it. Oh that God would open our eyes, and enable us to seize the prize so freely offered to every one of us!

But now we come to the *Third* point, and that a very interesting one.

Both Parables represent the person discovering the treasure, as *parting with all he has*, in order to possess it. "The kingdom of heaven is like unto a treasure hid in a field; the which, when a man hath found, he hideth, *and for joy thereof goeth and selleth all that he hath, and buyeth the field.* Again, the kingdom of heaven is like unto a Merchantman seeking goodly pearls, who when he hath found one pearl of great price, went and *sold all that he had, and bought it.*"

You see, the Treasure-finder, though for a while he keeps the discovery to himself, presently goes and *disposes of all he is worth*, that he may possess the treasure, and make it his. Again, the Pearl-seeker does the same—so anxious is he not to lose the precious object which is within his reach.

And is it any wonder, Brethren, when Heaven is our prize, and Christ our treasure, that we are sometimes called upon to give up much to obtain them? Is it any wonder that the Apostles and early Christians were required to leave "houses, and brethren, and sisters, and lands," for Christ's sake? Yes, and they even felt an inward joy in parting with them. It is said of some, that they "*took joyfully* the spoiling of their goods, knowing in themselves that they had in heaven a better and an enduring substance." Hear too how St. Paul speaks: he says, "What things were gain to me, those I counted loss for Christ. Yea doubtless, and I count all things but loss for the excellency of the knowledge of Christ Jesus my Lord, for whom I have suffered the loss of all things, and do count them but dung that I may win Christ."

And such too has been the experience of many of God's children. A wise Christian writer, who lived many hundred years ago, St. Augustine, speaking of his own conversion, tells us how easy he found it, through this joy, to give up all those pleasures of sin, to which he had once clung so closely. "How sweet," he says, "did it at once become to me to be without the sweetness of those toys; and what I dreaded to be parted from, was now a joy to part with. Thou, who art sweeter than all pleasure, Thou didst cast them forth, that instead thereof Thou mightest enter in Thyself."

Thank God, we hear of men giving up the dearest things they have, so as to make this one treasure their own. The thing parted with may be very different in one case to what it is in another. The ungodly man will have to part with his sin. The lover of money will have to give up his covetousness. The indolent man, his ease. The lover of pleasure, his gay company. The learned man, the wisdom he trusted in. The self-righteous man, his own goodness. Each must sell what he has, that he may gain the treasure. He *must* sell them; and yet I would rather say, He *willingly* sells them—as our Lord says in the Parable, "*For joy thereof* he goeth and selleth all that he hath." There is no force needed, and no compulsion necessary. The Christian cheerfully gives up all. What are my sins (he says), or my gains, or my good name among men, or my fancied righteousness? These are all brittle reeds, which will break from under me. They are but "filthy rags," that will not cover me. I will cast them all away. Let them perish—that I may possess Christ, and be found in Him!

Have you and I parted with all—yes, all that we are commanded to give up for Christ's sake—all that stands in the way between us and Him—all that interferes with our salvation? It is hard, I know, to do so. But we shall never win Christ, never possess Him, till we have done it. It is hard for flesh and blood. Our wicked, world-loving, hearts grudge to part with what has been dear to us. But God can make us willing, cheerfully willing, to strip ourselves of everything, that we may grasp so great a treasure.

But much as these Parables are alike, there is, as we have remarked, *one point of difference* between them. In the first Parable the man stumbles unexpectedly upon the treasure, without even looking for it. In the other the merchant seeks diligently, and then his search is rewarded by his finding a most precious pearl.

Our Lord must have purposely intended by this to shew how different Christians come into possession of gospel blessings.

Some are brought to Christ suddenly, unexpectedly, and without any preparation for it. Some are awakened in the midst of their sin and thoughtlessness, and are won over by God's exceeding grace. The Lord said concerning the Gentiles, "I was found of them that sought me not." "The people that walked in darkness have seen a great light: they that dwell in the land of the shadow of death, upon them hath the light shined." Saul, the persecutor, suddenly found the treasure, when, so far from seeking for it, he was rushing in the very opposite direction. The woman of Samaria, mentioned in John iv., is another instance. She little thought of lighting on the hid treasure, when she came to draw water at the well. And are there not instances, within our own knowledge, where "sin has abounded," and yet grace has "much more abounded"?

But these are extraordinary cases—unusual cases. *Most* Christians, like the pearl merchant, after much seeking, at length find eternal life. This is God's rule, "He that *seeketh* findeth, and to him that *knocketh* it shall be opened." The Ethiopian Eunuch, for instance, was reading the Scriptures—he was searching in the field, when Philip pointed out to him Christ the "hid treasure." Cornelius had been long feeling after the truth, when at length God sent Peter to reveal it to him. He had been a seeker of goodly pearls, and at length found one of great price.

What an unspeakable mercy it is if, by any means, we are led by the Holy Spirit to discover Christ—to find salvation! Oh, what a treasure it is, if we can but lay hold of it. No matter what it cost us, if we can but make it ours. A man may pay too dear for *gold*, but not for this *Pearl of great price*. We may be poor in this world; but if we possess this treasure, we are unspeakably rich.

Let us lose no time. Our day is but a short one. The night is near; and that is but a bad time for searching. Seek Christ with all your hearts. Seek Him now. Seek Him in His ordinances. He is hid, as the milk in the breast, as the marrow in the bone, as the manna in the dew, as the honey in the honeycomb. "Sell that ye have. Provide yourselves bags which wax not old, a treasure in the heavens that faileth not."

THE FISHING-NET.

MATT. XIII. 47—50.

"The kingdom of heaven is like unto a net, that was cast into the sea, and gathered of every kind: which, when it was full, they drew to shore, and sat down, and gathered the good into vessels, but cast the bad away. So shall it be at the end of the world: the angels shall come forth, and sever the wicked from among the just. And shall cast them into the furnace of fire: there shall be wailing and gnashing of teeth."

THE gathering of men into Christ's Church is here compared by our Lord to what is done by a Net. The Net is let down, and cast into the sea—that is, the Gospel is proclaimed in the world; and men are gathered into Christ's kingdom by it, as Fish are enclosed by a Net. Of those who are thus enclosed, some are good and some are bad; some amply repay the labours of the fisher, and some are utterly worthless.

But let us take the Parable piece by piece.

The comparison of a Net was a very suitable one at the time when our Lord spoke it, for He was then near the Sea of Gennesaret; and perhaps many a little fishing-boat was in sight, engaged in its busy work. This same idea was in His mind on another occasion, when, as He saw Andrew and Simon one day casting their net into the sea, He said, "Follow me, and I will make you *fishers of men.*"

In the Parable before us, then, our Lord compares the Gospel to a Net; and if we consider a little, we shall see that this comparison was a most fitting one.

First—No means are *so effectual* for catching fish as a Net. Other means are used; but none are so effectual as this. So the Preaching of the Gospel is the great means of gathering souls into the Church, and bringing them to Christ. He uses other means, but this is the chief. Our Lord's command to His disciples was, "Preach the Gospel." And St. Paul speaks of "the preaching of the cross" as "the power of God."

Every time a Minister preaches, he throws the Gospel net. He throws it in faith, according to the Lord's command, and looks to

Him for a blessing. Nor does he stop there. He is a fisher of men *at all times.* Wherever he may be, his work is to cast the Gospel net so as to enclose as many as he can within the folds of salvation, and to bring lost ones to the shore of safety.

Secondly—The Fisherman's success depends upon *the skill which he employs.* The Net, as it lies in the boat, is useless. As long as it remains there, no fish are gathered.

So the Gospel must be *set forth.* It must be *preached.* The word must be *spoken* in men's ears, and applied to their hearts. It is not enough that you sit at home, and read your Bible. It is well to do this. But something more is needed. It is God's will that His Word should be *heard.* "Faith cometh by *hearing.*" And why is this? I answer, such is His will. "It pleased God by the foolishness of preaching to save them that believe."

Some people set a higher value on the Sermon than they do on the Prayers. But this is clearly wrong; for what can be more important than for needy sinners to draw near to a God of mercy? But still, how immensely important is preaching! By it souls are won, and sinners saved. By it men are brought upon their knees, and are taught the value of prayer.

But I said something about *Skill*. Skill is needed for the fisherman; for if the net is cast into the sea by unskilful hands, the labour is in vain. And is not skill also needed in throwing the Gospel net? It is written, "He that winneth souls is wise." Oh, it needs the highest wisdom, and the greatest skill, to catch men. Our Lord's charge to the first preachers of His Gospel was, "Be ye wise as serpents." And St. Paul says, "Being crafty, I caught ye with guile." God forbid that we should exalt man's wisdom. I know that learning alone will not make a man an able minister of Christ. St. Paul tells us that "God hath chosen the foolish things of the world to confound the wise, and the weak things of the world to confound the things which are mighty, that no flesh should glory in his presence." And the Apostle says of himself, "I came among you not with excellency of speech or of wisdom. For I determined not to know anything among you, save Jesus

Christ and him crucified. And my speech and my preaching were not with enticing words of man's wisdom, but in demonstration of the Spirit and of power." Still ministers must act wisely. They must bring all their skill to bear. They are called upon to explain the deep things of God—to point out the way to heaven. "The priest's lips (says Malachi) should keep knowledge." And Solomon tells us, in the Book of Ecclesiastes, "Because the Preacher was wise, he sought to find out acceptable words."

Ever pray then for your Minister, that he may be endued with the Holy Spirit, and thus be a successful preacher—that he may throw the net skilfully and rightly—that he may draw numbers into it, and win many souls to Christ. How was it that St. Peter, when he let down his net on the day of Pentecost, gathered three thousand souls for Christ? It was because the Holy Spirit was poured out in large measure; and such power was given to the Preacher's words, that hearts were touched, and souls awakened. May a like power accompany the preaching of God's Word in the present day!

Thirdly—The fishing-net *sinks into the water*. And does not the Gospel reach down to the lowest depths of our fallen nature? Is there any one so far gone, so low, so utterly degraded, that he is beyond the reach of the Gospel? Does it not announce salvation to the very uttermost? Ah, there are some who were once plunged into the depths of sin; but the Gospel came to them with power, rescued them, and brought them to Christ. Thank God, the very lowest are sometimes reached, and then are lifted up to the very shore of heaven.

Fourthly—The net is let down *at a venture*, sometimes on one side of the boat, and sometimes on the other—sometimes almost in vain, and sometimes with much success.

Such is the work of those who labour for souls. They cast the net in faith, not knowing what the effect will be. Yes, and sometimes, when they least expect it, their success is greatest.

Once when our Lord came to His disciples as they were on the sea, He commanded them, saying, "Launch out into the deep, and let down your nets for a draught." This seemed like a hard command; for they had been working for some hours, and all to no purpose. But they dared not distrust Him. "Master, we have toiled all the night and have taken nothing; nevertheless at thy word we will let down the net." They did let it down; and immediately inclosed a great multitude of fishes.

Just so it is with Christ's ministers now. It is their duty to labour; but they know not when or where their labour may be blest.

Fifthly—The place where the net is cast is *the wide sea*—not some narrow river, but the wide sea. This reminds us that the Gospel is for *the world*. Wherever there are lost souls, it is to be sounded—not in a narrow corner of our land, for instance; but through the length and breadth of it—not in one country merely, but in all the world. This is the will of our heavenly Master. This is His gracious purpose, that the Gospel should be preached "to every creature." Our duty clearly is to spread the knowledge of Christ throughout the earth.

Salvation! O salvation!
  The joyful sound proclaim,
Till each remotest nation
  Has learnt Messiah's name.

Waft, waft, ye winds, His story,
  And you, ye waters, roll,
Till, like a sea of glory,
  It spreads from pole to pole.

Sixthly—A *troubled* sea—a storm—often brings in large shoals of fish. They cannot be taken perhaps *during* the actual raging of the tempest, but *afterwards* the time is often specially favourable.

And when do we win the most souls? Is it not often when God brings trouble among us—in the hour of trial—in the day of adversity? When all goes well with us, we are very apt to harden our hearts, and close our ears. God sees this, and is pleased in mercy to send affliction. Then men are aroused from their state of slumber, and begin to listen. Yes, it is at such times that the Gospel comes with a living force, and draws souls within the Saviour's Church.

Seventhly—The Net *takes the fish out of*

their natural element, where they live, and love to be. So the Gospel takes sinners out of that element, where they have long lived and loved to live. It brings them out of their sins, their evil practices, their worldly ways. It changes the very heart, and makes men "new creatures."

Once more—The Net takes fish *of every kind*, some great, some small—some good, and some worthless. And so does the Gospel Net. It gathers of every sort—some rich, some poor; some great ones, some little ones who are despised in the eyes of the world. There is a saying that "they are not all fish that come to the net." So those are not all true Believers, who are gathered into Christ's Church. Some prove to be "foolish virgins," mere professors, having the name of godliness, without the power.

Thus we see how admirably this comparison of the Net shows us what the Gospel does in bringing men into Christ's kingdom.

But there are two or three points of *differ-*

ence which may well be noticed, between the fisherman's work, and the work of Christ's ministers.

1. The fish are always taken *against their will*. They swim blindly into the snare. But no man was ever compelled to come to Christ. Grace *draws* us: it never *forces* us. God makes His people willing. He overcomes their unbelief; and they yield themselves to Him heartily, readily, cheerfully.

2. Again, the fish are caught to be *destroyed, or devoured*. But men are laid hold of by the Gospel, that they may be saved.

3. Again, the fisher's *net may break*. Some of its meshes may be weak, and worn out. But "the word of the Lord endureth for ever." It needs no mending. It cannot be broken. "The law of the Lord is perfect," says David, "converting the soul. The testimony of the Lord is sure, making wise the simple."

There is yet one more thing, which I wish you to bear in mind. There is another Net, and other Fishers, besides the Gospel of Christ and His ministers. Satan is ever fishing for men. He casts his net in all directions. He spreads it secretly for unwary souls. Nay, at the very time when the Gospel net is being cast, he is not idle. His net is being cast too. Bad thoughts, worldly thoughts, trifling thoughts, are being suggested. Whilst Christ's ministers preach, he is not a mere looker-on. He is preaching too. He is calling you another way. He is trying to persuade you not to come to the Saviour, but to enjoy sin a little longer. Take care that you fall not into *his* snare.

Thus, I have shown you, in what respects the Gospel resembles a net, and in what respects it differs from it.

The Parable further teaches us much that we learnt in the Parable of the Tares.

There the Tares and Wheat grew together. *Here* the good and bad fish are collected in the same net. In both Parables *a separation time* is mentioned. The Tares are gathered out, when Harvest comes: the worthless Fish are cast away, when the net is drawn to shore.

Both point to that great day of meeting and of parting—of assembling and dividing—when

God shall send forth His angels to gather together His elect, and to banish for ever the ungodly from His presence.

That day is not yet come; but it *will* come. Now is the time of mercy. Now is the day of salvation. The Gospel net, in these days, is thrown further and wider than it was ever thrown before. Souls are being gathered in. Oh, that many may be brought safe to shore, and may be found among Christ's true people in the great day of His appearing!

THE UNFORGIVING SERVANT.

MATT. XVIII. 23—35.

"Therefore is the kingdom of heaven likened unto a certain king, which would take account of his servants. And when he had begun to reckon, one was brought unto him, which owed him ten thousand talents. But forasmuch as he had not to pay, his lord commanded him to be sold, and his wife, and children, and all that he had, and payment to be made. The servant therefore fell down, and worshipped him, saying, Lord, have patience with me, and I will pay thee all. Then the lord of that servant was moved with compassion, and loosed him, and forgave him the debt. But the same servant went out, and found one of his fellowservants, which owed him an hundred pence: and he laid hands on him, and took him by the throat, saying, Pay me that thou owest. And his fellowservant fell down at his feet, and besought him, saying, Have patience with me, and I will pay thee all. And he would not: but went and cast him into prison, till he should pay the debt. So when his fellowservants saw what was done, they were very sorry, and came and told unto their lord all that was done. Then his lord, after that he had called him, said unto him, O thou wicked servant, I forgave thee all that debt, because thou desiredst me; shouldest not thou also have had compassion on thy fellowservant, even as I had pity on thee? And his lord was wroth, and delivered him to the tormentors, till he should pay all that was due unto him. So likewise shall my heavenly Father do also unto you, if ye from your hearts forgive not every one his brother their trespasses."

WHAT was it that led our Lord to speak this Parable? A question of St. Peter's led to it. And this question again was asked, in consequence of some words which Jesus had been speaking. If you look into the chapter, you will see, in ver. 13, that our Lord tells us what we should do, if one of our brethren should trespass against us—that we should first take him aside, and tell him of his fault *privately;* and that, if this fails, we must deal more openly with him, and bring the matter before the Church. This leads St. Peter to ask, in ver. 21, "Lord, *how oft* shall my brother sin against me, and I forgive him? Till *seven* times?" This, even, was more than the

Jewish teachers required. They advised the forgiveness of *three* offences. Peter, however, names "seven," feeling perhaps that under the Gospel law of love a larger, freer, and fuller forgiveness was called for.

Now, observe what our Lord recommends. He goes farther still—"I say not unto thee, Until seven times: but, Until *seventy times seven.*" And then He puts the matter powerfully before him in the shape of a Parable.

He describes a certain King, who had under him a great many servants—some probably holding high offices in his kingdom, and some waiting upon him in his palace. One of these, evidently a person of some importance, owes him a very large sum—ten thousand talents— that is, about three million pounds of our money. Being utterly unable to pay this enormous debt, he throws himself upon his Master's compassion. He "falls down, and worships him," that is, he humbles himself before him, and intreats him not to imprison him for life, or sell him as a bondman, which was the punishment due to him. His Master not only listens patiently to what he has to say, but receives him with the utmost kindness, frees him from his confinement, and forgives him all the debt.

It so happens that this pardoned servant has a small sum owing to him from one of his fellow-servants. It is only a hundred pence, or about three pounds in our money—a mere trifle compared with what *he* himself had owed. But he sternly demands payment. And because he did not receive it at once, he seizes the poor debtor, and, in spite of his earnest entreaties, casts him into prison.

As soon as this comes to the Master's ears, he immediately summons the unthankful servant into his presence, upbraids him for his hardheartedness and ingratitude, and punishes him as he deserves.

Such is the Story: now for the Interpretation.

Who is the "certain King"? It is God Himself, the great King of kings, and Lord of lords. And who is the servant who owed the ten thousand talents? It is you and I, whose debts are so great, and who deserve, each one of us, to be cast into the eternal prison of hell. The King's conduct towards his servant is a picture of God's love and mercy to us sinners, freely forgiving the penitent, although he has nothing whatever to offer for his sins.

Then, the cruel conduct of the Servant towards his fellow-servant is to show us the hatefulness of an unforgiving spirit towards a brother, when God has been so patient and so gracious towards us.

What a blessed subject for us to dwell upon—Forgiveness! The Forgiveness which the penitent believer receives from God, and the Forgiveness which he ought to be ever ready to bestow on his offending brother.

1. The Forgiveness which the penitent believer has received from God.

He is a forgiven man. How is this? It is true, we all owe a debt, a heavy debt, to God. David knew the vastness of this debt, when he said, in Ps. xl., "Mine iniquities have taken hold upon me, so that I am not able to look up: they are more than the hairs of mine head; therefore my heart faileth me."

And again, in Ps. xix., he exclaims, "Who can understand his errors?"—or, as our Prayer-book translation has it, "Who can tell how oft he offendeth?" Think of all our shortcomings, and all our ill-doings. Think of all we have left undone, and all we have done amiss. Think of all our evil thoughts, all our idle words, all our unworthy acts. Think of the sins we committed long ago in our youth, or lately in our riper years; the bad deeds done in the days of our ignorance, and those which have stained our lives, since we have known something of God and of His love. What debts there are standing against us in the book of heaven! Truly we are debtors before God—utterly miserable, hopeless, helpless!

And is it not true also that, like the Servant in the Parable, we have nothing to pay off these enormous debts with—absolutely nothing? We are penniless. We have not a farthing to give. We cannot pay even a particle of our debt. Our mis-spent time, for instance, that we have frittered away, which should have been given to God—how can we ever make amends for that? The harm we have done in the world; the injury we have caused perhaps to a brother's soul by our bad example; the talents we have wasted; the opportunities lost; the laws of God which we have trampled upon—not one of these can we undo or recal.

But the Debtor in the Parable beseeches his Master to give him time, and the debt shall be discharged; "Have patience with me, and I will pay thee all." This was utterly impossible. He could *never* pay it. But in the fear and anguish of the moment, he is ready to promise anything, so that he may be delivered from his present danger.

And the awakened sinner, when the wrath of an offended God seems to press home upon him, is apt to fancy that he can himself pay off his debt—that he can at all events do something towards the repayment. But no; he has nothing to offer, nothing to give. He must come, simply craving mercy—as a criminal, pleading before God. It is true, he may do better in future; but he cannot undo what has been already done. If it were possible for us to lead a perfectly sinless life from this hour, our future holiness would not atone for past transgressions—not one spot could it wash out from our sin-stained souls.

What we need is Forgiveness. This is what a sinner longs for, the moment he feels the greatness of his debt, and the hopelessness of his case. Then he anxiously inquires where pardon is to be found. He opens his Bible, and there, to his great joy, he discovers that God delighteth in mercy—that there is forgiveness with Him. Did he never know this before? Yes, he knew it all along, but never in the way that he knows it now.

A pardoning God! This is the very thing we want. Salvation for the lost! This is the very boon to meet our case. A Saviour, who has bled for us—who has died for the ungodly—who has paid the debtor's due, the ten thousand talents, when he could not pay one of them himself! Here is grace, far surpassing all our deserts.

Let me ask, Has God convinced you of your debt? Has He showed you that you are a hopeless bankrupt, deserving only to be cast away, and that for ever? Has He drawn from your lips an earnest cry for mercy?

And further—have you found that mercy for yourself—found it in the cross—found it in the blood that cleanseth from all sin? Then you can indeed speak of the blessedness of "the man, whose unrighteousness is forgiven, and whose sin is covered."

But, you observe, that the King, in the Parable, treated his debtor with a little severity at first: he "commanded him to be sold, and his wife, and children, and all that he had, and payment to be made."

Now, are we to gather from this, that God is harsh and severe—that He is "extreme to mark what is done amiss?" No; He is a God, full of love. Before we ever turn to Him, His eye of mercy is towards us. He "waiteth to be gracious." Like a Father, He listens for the first cry of His returning children. But we may learn this—that God hates sin; and, so long as the sinner remains impenitent, he is treasuring up for himself wrath against the day of wrath: God is angry with him every day.

So much for the first part of the Parable,

which is intended to describe the forgiveness which the penitent believer has received from God. It is a full, a free, an entire forgiveness of all his sins. God looks upon the debt, as if it had never existed.

But let us go on a step, and see what the Parable teaches, as to our being ever *ready to forgive an offending brother.* It is clearly our duty, as Christians, to forgive. Without it, what can we expect? where is our hope? It is written, "He shall have judgment without mercy, that showed no mercy." "Forgive," says our Lord, "and ye shall be forgiven." "Be merciful, even as your Father which is in heaven is merciful." And what is the petition which most of us put up every day of our lives? "Our Father, forgive us our trespasses, as we forgive them that trespass against us,"—that is, "Forgive us, just in the same degree that we forgive others." If then you are an unforgiving one, only see what your prayer amounts to:—" O God, I have not forgiven my brother; I cannot forgive him: *therefore* do not forgive me—let me also remain unforgiven." What an awful prayer! And yet, so long as you are unforgiving, you put up this very prayer day by day.

Now, one would think that a Christian, to whom mercy has been shown, would at least feel mercy for others—that, having been forgiven himself, he would be ever ready to forgive his brother. Is it so? Alas! if we look around us, there are too many proofs that this spirit of forgiveness and long-suffering is sadly wanting, even among Christ's people. There was need then of the latter part of the Parable, as well as the first part.

But you will say, "It is hard to bring ourselves to forgive." Yes, I know it is hard. For our wicked hearts love to take revenge. Our proud hearts will not stoop to pass by injuries. And, in this respect, what a difference there is between God and men. When *we* forgive, it costs us an effort: but *God* delighteth in showing mercy.

In Luke xvii., Jesus says to His disciples, "If thy brother trespass against thee, rebuke him; and if he repent, forgive him. And if he trespass against thee seven times in a day, and seven times in a day turn again to thee, saying, I repent, thou shalt forgive him." When Jesus said this, His disciples exclaimed, "Lord, increase our faith!" They felt how difficult it was to carry out this loving precept, and so they asked that more faith might be given them from above.

Yes, it is hard to forgive our brother, if he has wronged us—I mean, *completely* to forgive him. We will forgive him in part, but not entirely—not all the debt. We will forgive him perhaps, *if he will humble himself* before us, and own himself wrong. This will be some amends to us: it will satisfy our pride. Or we will forgive him *in words*, so that nothing more is required of us. We will *say* that we bear him no ill-will; for this will not cost us much. But our Lord requires more; for He speaks, at the close of the Parable, of *heart*-forgiveness being necessary: "If ye *from your hearts* forgive not."

Let us ask God, then, to grant us a forgiving heart—such a patient, tender, loving spirit as Jesus has shown to us.

It is hard, I say, to forgive—hard for flesh

and blood—hard, unless grace has gained the victory in our hearts. But if our unforgiving temper has been subdued, and a Christ-like spirit has been given us, then how sweet it is, how blessed, to shew mercy to others!

Was that Servant happy, when he went out and cast his fellow-servant into prison? And are you happy, when you bear malice in your heart against a neighbour? Can you be really happy, when you know that there is in this wide world even *one*, whom you cannot look upon with a feeling of kindness and love?

Oh, there is a joy in forgiveness. What joy there would be in going to the prison cell of some Debtor, with a pardon in your hand; and especially if you could say, "I know myself what it is to have been a prisoner. I have tasted the sweets of liberty." Truly there is a joy in forgiving. Then let us not shut ourselves out from that joy. Let us taste often of that happiness, by cultivating a spirit of forgiveness towards all around us.

Try and carry out in your daily life the lessons which Jesus teaches us in this Parable. If there is any one who has wronged you, heartily forgive him. If you have borne any secret illwill in your heart, immediately put it away. If there is any malice or bad feeling, lurking like a little grain of poison in a hidden corner of your bosom, at once cast it out.

Call to mind often your own guilt, and what a gracious God has done for you. Constantly think of His tender mercy towards you. This will prevent you from being harsh and unfeeling. This will keep your heart right. This will make you "kind one to another, tenderhearted, forgiving one another, even as God for Christ's sake hath forgiven you."

THE LABOURERS IN THE VINEYARD.

MATT. xx. 1—16.

"For the kingdom of heaven is like unto a man that is an householder, which went out early in the morning to hire labourers into his vineyard. And when he had agreed with the labourers for a penny a day, he sent them into his vineyard. And he went out about the third hour, and saw others standing idle in the marketplace, and said unto them: Go ye also into the vineyard, and whatsoever is right I will give you. And they went their way. Again he went out about the sixth and ninth hour, and did likewise. And about the eleventh hour he went out, and found others standing idle, and saith unto them, Why stand ye here all the day idle? They say unto him, Because no man hath hired us. He saith unto them, Go ye also into the vineyard; and whatsoever is right, that shall ye receive. So when even was come, the lord of the vineyard saith unto his steward, Call the labourers, and give them their hire, beginning from the last unto the first. And when they came that were hired about the eleventh hour, they received every man a penny. But when the first came they supposed that they should have received more; and they

THE LABOURERS IN THE VINEYARD. 93

likewise received every man a penny. And when they had received it, they murmured against the goodman of the house, saying, These last have wrought but one hour, and thou hast made them equal unto us, which have borne the burden and heat of the day. But he answered one of them, and said, Friend, I do thee no wrong: didst thou not agree with me for a penny? Take that thine is, and go thy way: I will give unto this last, even as unto thee. Is it not lawful for me to do what I will with mine own? Is thine eye evil, because I am good? So the last shall be first, and the first last: for many be called, but few chosen."

THE Parable which is now before us is certainly not one of the easiest. There are difficulties about it, which require much thought and consideration.

Let us do what I recommended in the beginning of this Book—namely, look back a little, and see if we can find *anything which led to the Parable;* for, if so, this will greatly help us to understand it.

Now, in the foregoing chapter, the nineteenth, we read of a Young Ruler coming to Jesus, with an earnest enquiry as to how he could obtain eternal life. And upon our Lord proposing to him to give up his riches, to which he was evidently clinging too closely, he went away with a downcast look and a sorrowful heart.

Upon this Peter puts a question to the Saviour, "Behold, *we* have forsaken all, and followed thee. What shall we have therefore?" Jesus assures him that such should indeed receive an ample reward. "But," he adds at the close of the chapter, "many that are first shall be last, and the last shall be first." That is to say, many who seem to be the first and foremost are not so in God's estimate. Then follows the Parable.

Now, there was clearly something wrong lurking in Peter's mind, when he asked the question; and that led our Lord to speak the Parable. You see, Peter wished to know what *their* reward should be, who had done the very thing which the Young Ruler was so unwilling to do—who had forsaken all for the gospel's sake. The question, "What shall we have therefore," was not quite a right one. It was putting their devotedness to Christ on a wrong footing. It was as if they were making a sort of calculation—so much work, so much reward. There was a comparing of themselves with that young man, who felt the Saviour's proposal too hard for him.

Now let us examine the Parable.

Here is a certain Householder, or, as we should say, a certain Occupier of Land, who possesses among his other fields a Vineyard. These Vineyards required much the same kind of cultivation as we give to our Hop-gardens. The ground was dug in the Spring time, and care was taken to keep them clear of weeds. Then, at the end of the summer, when the gathering time came, many hands were needed to pick the grapes.

At one of these busy seasons, the Householder goes to the most likely place to find labourers, namely, into the market-place of the neighbouring village or town.

He first goes out at daybreak, and engages some. He promises to give them a penny for their day's work, which is about eight-pence of our money. And they agree to his terms, and go into the vineyard.

Finding he wants more labourers, he goes

again at the third hour, that is, about nine o'clock, and hires more.

In the afternoon he goes again, and still finds several unemployed. These too he sends into his vineyard.

At length, when it only wants an hour of dusk, he makes a last visit to the market-place. And finding some even then not at work, he sends them to join the others, promising to give them whatever is right.

When the day closed, and evening set in, the Owner called his Steward, or Bailiff, to him, and desired him to pay the labourers, beginning with those who had come last into the vineyard. To each man the same payment was made. A penny was given to the last, as well as to the first.

Now, this caused great discontentment among those who had been at work all the day. It seemed to them that the Master had not acted fairly towards them, since *they* had worked longer for him than their brethren. They said, "These have wrought but one hour, and thou hast made them equal unto us, which have borne the burden and heat of the day."

The Master, in reply, reminds them that he had promised them a certain sum, and *that* they had received. They had therefore nothing to complain of. And what, if he had given some *more* than their due? He had a right so to act; for the money was his own, and he had perfect liberty to bestow it as he pleased.

Now, it is rather difficult to see what is *the drift* of the Parable. But if we bear in mind St. Peter's question which he had asked, and also the remark that our Lord makes at the close of the Parable, we shall, I think, have the key that we want. Having spoken the Parable, Jesus says, just as He had said before, "So the last shall be first, and the first last"; and then He also adds, "For many be called, but few chosen."

The following then are the Lessons which the Parable teaches—

First, that men will not be rewarded hereafter merely for the *amount* of work which they have done for Christ. Neither will their reward depend on *length of service*. On the contrary, many who have in these respects been "last" will be accounted "first."

Secondly, that of those who are called into Christ's service, only a few are numbered among His true people now, and only a few will share His kingdom hereafter.

Let us now consider these two Lessons, just as our Lord put them.

The last shall be first, and the first last— this is one Lesson which the Parable teaches.

For instance, the *first in worldly rank* are often the very poorest according to God's estimate. Many a person who has been honoured here—who has been lifted up by station above the level of his fellow-men— or who has obtained a great name for his learning or for his valour—perhaps such an one may hereafter sink down into the lowest place, and even be altogether thrust out of God's kingdom.

Again, *the first in privilege and opportunities* may not stand so high in God's favour as some who have had much fewer advantages. The man who has lived in a Christian land, for example, with gospel light shining all around him, may be condemned hereafter, whilst some poor Heathen who has only just heard of the Saviour's name, but has fled to Him as His hope, may be accepted. The one may have professed to be a worker in God's vineyard all his life: the other may have been till very lately shut out from it altogether.

Or, we might take two persons living in the same Christian country. One may have had the advantage of education. He may be the child of pious parents. He may have been long watched over by a faithful Minister. And yet he may not have profited by these great opportunities. Whilst another, with much less light, and much fewer blessings, may have found Christ, and earnestly followed Him.

Again, there are some who are always *putting themselves first*—anxious to be noticed —desiring to take the lead—who have a good opinion of themselves, and wish others to have a good opinion of them—who, like the Pharisees, sound a trumpet before them. These will one day be thrown back into the shade, and be little esteemed by Him who looks into the heart; whilst, on the other hand, some meek, humble, lowly one will be exalted. He may be unknown, and even dishonoured now; but he will be acknowledged before the angels of God. He was content to take the lowest seat; but it shall be said to him, "Friend, come up higher."

Once more. Do we not occasionally see persons, who have begun early to serve God, fairly *outstripped by others who were brought later into the Lord's service?* Like the Labourers in the Parable, they entered the vineyard at the third hour; but perhaps they have grown dull and weary. Their faith has flagged; their love has cooled; and they are put to shame by some newly-awakened Christian whose heart burns with a holier zeal. Of such it may be truly said, "The last shall be first, and the first last."

Still there is not one word in the Parable to encourage *delay*—not one word that would lead us to suppose that it matters little *when* we enter upon the Lord's service. The whole of Scripture teaches us far otherwise. Do we not again and again find a blessing resting on early piety? And are we not exhorted *now* —*at once*—to live a Christian life?

The Parable encourages us to enter *heartily* on our work, whenever God calls us to it, in the happy assurance that our labour will not be in vain in the Lord. And further, it seems to warn us that, although we may *seem* to be first, if we are not watchful, we may fall back into the hindmost rank; and also that we should never boast, or consider the battle over, till we have gained the victory, and put off our armour.

So much for the first Lesson which the Parable teaches—"The last shall be first, and the first last."

And now for the other Lesson—*Many be called, but few chosen;* that is, there are many who are invited into the Lord's service, who are never accepted as His saved people.

The Jews, for instance, were *called* into God's kingdom. They were called by Moses and the Prophets, and afterwards by Christ Himself. But because they refused to receive Him, and to embrace His gospel, they were in the end rejected.

We too, who belong to the Christian Church, have been all *called.* We were called to serve Christ at our Baptism. We were called again at our Confirmation. We are called every time the house of God is open. And has not God sent some of us *special* calls besides? Alas, it will be found at the great day that many of us have been called, but few chosen.

Christ's true people are the *few*. They always have been the few out of the many, and they are so now. It will be of little use hereafter to be among the "called." It will be but a poor argument to say, "Thou hast taught in our streets. We have heard of Thee every Sabbath. Thy name was familiar to us." It will only add to our condemnation, and make our guilt tenfold greater. The gospel was brought very near to us; but we put it from us—we made light of it.

Such is the main teaching of the Parable. These are the two principal Lessons which, I think, our Lord wished us to learn from it. But there are three or four other things which may be noticed.

For instance, we may gather from the Parable that God has a work for us *all* to do; and woe be unto us, if we pass through life without doing it!

Then, observe some of the men in the Parable saying, "*No man hath hired us.*" Now, there is not one of *us* who can say that. You and I shall have no such excuse to offer. God has taken us into His service. Nay, have we not *pledged ourselves* to serve Him faithfully? Oh, if we have neglected our Master's work, let us go back to it. There are only twelve short hours in our working day. Perhaps three, six, or even eleven of those precious hours may be gone for ever. The night is soon coming, when no man can work.

Further, we may observe that some of these Labourers, who were taken early into the Vineyard, *murmured because the same kindness was shewn to their brethren who were hired later.* Beware of this feeling. Like a fly in the ointment, it will spoil your work. There should be no grudging, no jealousy, among Christ's people. Are any honoured more than we? Be it so. At any rate we have more—far more—than we deserve. "Let nothing be done through strife or vainglory; but in lowliness of mind let each esteem other better than themselves."

Lastly, the Master said to his Labourers, "Whatsoever is *right* I will give you." And so God says to us. To one He gives health, and strength, and riches : to another sickness, trials, and poverty. Be content; He gives what is *right*. Let us be thankful for what He *denies* us, as well as for what He *grants* us. Be assured, whatever comes is the *right* thing for us. And what matters it, if He withholds from us this or that earthly blessing, so long as He gives us His own dear Son, and salvation through Him?

May God give us thankful and contented hearts, convinced that we deserve nothing at His hands, and feeling that if we reach heaven at last, it will not be because we have earned it, but because God has given it to us of His free love and mercy!

THE TWO SONS.

MATT. XXI. 28—32.

"But what think ye? A certain man had two sons; and he came to the first, and said, Son, go work to day in my vineyard. He answered and said, I will not; but afterward he repented, and went. And he came to the second, and said likewise. And he answered and said, I go, sir: and went not. Whether of them twain did the will of his father? They say unto him, The first. Jesus saith unto them, Verily I say unto you, That the publicans and the harlots go into the kingdom of God before you. For John came unto you in the way of righteousness, and ye believed him not: but the publicans and the harlots believed him: and ye, when ye had seen it, repented not afterward, that ye might believe him."

WHEN an Army invades a Country, it has to make its way among enemies, who are most unwilling to receive it. It is sure therefore to meet with opposition at all points. Every step it takes is disputed.

When our Lord came into this world, it proved to be *an enemy's country*. Though He " came unto his own, his own received him not." The Jews set themselves against Him, and opposed Him at every step. What David foretold truly came to pass—" The heathen raged, and the people imagined a vain thing : the kings of the earth set themselves, and the rulers took counsel together, against the Lord, and against his Anointed." At one moment, they put a false meaning to His words; and at another, " they laid to His charge things that He knew not."

St. Matthew, in the chapter now before us, mentions that, on one occasion, as Jesus went into the Temple, the Chief Priests and Elders roughly questioned His claims as a Teacher— " By what authority doest thou these things ? and who gave thee this authority ? "

Our Lord meets this with much calmness and wisdom. He puts to them a question, which they evidently found a great difficulty in answering, " I also will ask you one thing, which, if ye tell me, I in like wise will tell you by what authority I do these things. The baptism of John, whence was it? from heaven, or of men?"

Now, He knew that this question would place them in the greatest difficulty; for, whatever answer they gave, they would convict themselves. If they replied, "From heaven," then He would immediately say to them, "Why did ye not then believe him?" And yet they dared not say, "Of men;" for this would have been in opposition to the general opinion of the people, for "all (that is, the great mass of men) held John as a prophet." And so "they answered Jesus and said, We cannot tell. And he said unto them, Neither tell I you by what authority I do these things." Thus He "took the wise in their own craftiness." And this it was which led Him to speak the Parable now before us.

There were two Sons, He says, whose Father possessed a Vineyard. He bids each of them to go and labour on his ground—"Son, work to-day in my vineyard." One of the Sons at first refuses; but afterwards he repents of his disobedience, and goes and does as his Father desired him. The other Son appears at first to be much more obedient. He answers, "I go, Sir;" but "went not."

And here our Lord wishes to describe two sorts of persons—some that *perform better than they promise*, and some that *promise better than they perform*.

The first Son, who for a while refused, but afterwards came to a better mind, represents the Publicans and Harlots, who, when our Lord came, were looked upon as worthless outcasts, making not even a profession of religion; but who (many of them) repented, embraced the gospel, and became believers in Christ. And the second Son, who made a show of obedience, represents those very Jews, who had just been attacking Him. They professed to love and obey God; but, when tried, were found sadly wanting.

Now, our Lord put it plainly to His opposers, and asked them, Which of the two, they thought, did the will of his father? And when He drew from them the acknowledgment that it was the first, He then went on to show them that the picture was intended to apply to *them*. They were like the second Son, who promised to work, but did not keep his word. Look at ver. 31:—"Jesus saith unto them, Verily I say unto you, That the publicans and the harlots go into the kingdom of God before you." They are more ready to receive Christ than you, who are kept back by your pride and self-righteousness. They are far more ready to bend their necks to the gospel yoke.

And then He thus explains Himself, "For John came unto you in the way of righteousness, and ye believed him not: but the publicans and the harlots believed him: and ye, when ye had seen it, repented not afterward, that ye might believe him."

It is true that a greater than John had now come—even Jesus Himself; and the great sin of the Jews consisted in rejecting *Him*. But our Lord is content to charge them with their guilt in refusing to receive *John*, who was His servant and His forerunner. And afterwards, when He, the Master, came, working miracles, and teaching as never man taught, they repented not, but also rejected *Him*.

Such was the Parable, and its meaning. It was spoken against the Jews who opposed

Christ; and on them our Lord effectually fastened it. But it may be also useful, very useful, to *us*. It has a word too for *our* ears, if we will but hear it.

1. Our Lord would teach us, that *profession without practice is displeasing to Him.* One of these sons professed to obey his father with the utmost readiness; but his actions did not correspond with his promises.

How easy it is to make a profession of religion! To be baptized, to come to God's house, to receive His ministers, to fall in with many of the practices of religious persons about us—all this is easy enough. But we may still be very far from the kingdom of God: we may still be outside the door, and may never enter in. The heart may not be touched. There may be no true love for Christ, no giving up of sin for His sake, no taking up the cross to follow Him. Judas made a profession, but he was no disciple. Simon the Sorcerer was baptized, and became a member of Christ's Church, and joined himself to the Apostles for a time; but he was all the while "in the gall of bitterness and in the bond of iniquity."

So it was with the Pharisees. They "*said*, and *did not*." Their character was well described by Isaiah (chap. xxix. 13) :—" This people draweth nigh unto me with their mouth, and honoureth me with their lips; but their heart is far from me."

And is there not a danger of *our* falling into the same snare—professing more than we feel, more than we believe, more than we are prepared to perform? I would rather see a person like Nicodemus, or Joseph of Arimathæa, who for a while kept himself in the shade, than like Jehu, who cried, " Come, see my zeal for the Lord."

Do not mistake me. We *ought* to make a profession, and we dishonour Christ if we shrink from it. But then let it be an honest, true-hearted profession ; and let our daily life be in keeping with it. Let us promise little, and do much. Let us not sound a trumpet before us, but let us try to do good secretly. Let us make no display with our lamps, but let us see that they give forth a clear light.

Oh for more of that inner work of God in our souls ! Oh, for more of the indwelling of the Spirit, filling us with holy light and love !

Oh that we may live unto God, and not unto men; and be able to say, with Peter, "Lord, thou knowest all things; thou knowest that I love thee"!

2. We may learn from this Parable that the *Penitent are welcome to Christ*. We know this from many other portions of Scripture; but here it is especially taught us.

Happy those who have *always* walked in God's ways, from their very childhood upwards—who have loved Him in their earliest and freshest days, and given Him their first and best affections. They are specially dear to Him now; and they will be greatly honoured hereafter. Their's will be a bright crown indeed.

But what of those, who have wandered and strayed from the right path? What, if for years they had no thought about their souls, and just walked in the ways of the world around them? Is any hope held out to *such?* Is there any way pointed out, by which *they* may return, and ·find forgiveness? Yes; there is mercy for the penitent. "We have an advocate with the Father, Jesus

Christ the righteous, and he is the propitiation for our sins." Like the repenting Son in the parable, our services may yet be accepted. There is pardon for the contrite sinner. There is salvation for the lost, through the abounding merits of the Saviour.

The Publicans and Harlots were bad enough; but, when they felt their sins, and sought for mercy in Christ, they found acceptance. The difference between them and the Pharisees was, as the difference which we sometimes see between two persons who are sick. In one, the disease is *in the frame*, but there is no *outward* symptom to be seen. In the other, the disease *shews itself*, and takes a decided shape. The last is far the most hopeful of the two, and is the most likely to come to the Physician to be cured.

Oh the riches of God's patience and mercy, in having borne so long with us! And oh the depth of His love, in receiving back the penitent and contrite sinner, and granting him a place among His children!

Be encouraged by this Parable to go and lay down your sins at the cross, and seek pardon through the Saviour's precious blood.

Go now, while the door is open; or it may be too late to seek an entrance. It has been well said, that "a late repentance is seldom true," but that "true repentance never comes too late."

3. Another thing which the Parable reminds us of is, that *God bids us all to work for Him.* He says to you and me, "Son, work in my vineyard." We must not be content with talking and feeling; but we must *work* for Him. He has done so much for us, that we owe Him all our strength, and all our service. And most assuredly, if our hearts are influenced by His grace, we shall feel a longing desire to be *doing* something for Him. By the sin of Adam we were turned out, as it were, to labour in the barren world; but by grace we are called again to work in our Father's vineyard: and that is profitable, pleasant, happy work. To do His will— to serve Him during our few short days on earth—to be doing something which is pleasing and acceptable to Him—this is our duty and our privilege. May we be ever ready to be so employed!

4. But lastly, we are reminded also that we must *enter upon our work at once.* There must be no delay, no putting off till to-morrow—" Son, work *to-day* in my vineyard."

Ah, dear Friends, our time is slipping away very quickly. If some of us could count our remaining years, or even weeks, we should find them to be very few; and yet there is much to be done. Are we doing it ? Long enough, and earnestly enough, we have done the world's work—and perhaps Satan's work too. Oh that we may employ the little time that is left in working for our heavenly Master!

Perhaps we have been labouring hard for some object, which in a few years we shall feel to be of but little importance : and we shall then wonder that we worked for it with such eagerness. Perhaps we have been striving to gain something that we must soon lose again. We have indeed been "spending our money for that which is not bread, and our labour for that which satisfieth not." Oh let us now give ourselves to God, to spend, and be spent, in His service. Let us be doing that work now, in which we should like to be found occupied at our Lord's coming.

THE WICKED HUSBANDMEN.

MARK XII. 1—12.

"And he began to speak unto them by parables. A certain man planted a vineyard, and set an hedge about it, and digged a place for the wine-fat, and built a tower, and let it out to husbandmen, and went into a far country. And at the season he sent to the husbandmen a servant, that he might receive from the husbandmen of the fruit of the vineyard. And they caught him, and beat him, and sent him away empty. And again he sent unto them another servant; and at him they cast stones, and wounded him in the head, and sent him away shamefully handled. And again he sent another; and him they killed, and many others; beating some, and killing some. Having yet therefore one son, his well-beloved, he sent him also last unto them, saying, They will reverence my son. But those husbandmen said among themselves, This is the heir; come, let us kill him, and the inheritance shall be ours. And they took him, and killed him, and cast him out of the vineyard. What shall therefore the lord of the vineyard do? he will come and destroy the husbandmen, and will give the vineyard unto others. And have ye not read this scripture, The stone which the builders rejected is become the head of the corner: this was the Lord's doing, and it is marvellous in our eyes? And they sought to lay hold on him, but feared the people; for they knew that he had spoken the parable against them: and they left him, and went their way."

(See also Matt. xxi. 33—44; Luke xx. 9—18.)

St. Luke tells us that this Parable was delivered in the hearing of the Chief Priests and Scribes; and that they soon saw that it was spoken against *them.*

Here again we have a Vineyard, as we had in the last Parable. And the Owner of it is described as making a Hedge round it; and a Wine-fat, that is, a place in which the grapes are pressed; and also a Tower, for the purpose of keeping watch against intruders. Having planted it, and let it out to certain Husbandmen, he goes away for a time; and at the proper season he sends one of his servants to see that all is going on well, and to receive a portion of the grapes, by way of rent.

The first messenger who goes is ill-treated, and returns empty-handed. Another and another is sent; and each fares worse than the one who went before him. These wicked Husbandmen were not content with wronging their Landlord, but they also vented their rage upon his servants, beating some, and killing others.

At length the Master, having a favourite Son—an only Son—and one whom he greatly loved—determined to send him, saying, "They will reverence my Son. However they may have treated others, it may be, they will respect *him*." But no; for no sooner do they see him coming, than they exclaim, "This is the heir: let us kill him, that the inheritance may be ours." And forthwith they follow up their threat, and put him to death.

It is not difficult to see what our Lord meant by this Parable.

First, He meant to describe the wicked conduct of *the Jews*, especially as regards their treatment of Himself. And, no doubt, He intended also to shew us *our* sin, if we reject the message of salvation which He has sent us.

Let us see how exactly the conduct of *the*

Jews is here described. Their nation was like this Vineyard of which He speaks. The greatest pains had been taken with them. No people were so cared for, as they had been from the very first. And yet no people made so bad a return for all the mercy bestowed upon them.

When for instance they were suffering in Egypt, the Lord sent Moses to deliver them, to declare His will to them, and to be their guide to the Promised Land. But how unthankful were they for this great blessing! They murmured against their Deliverer, and at times were almost disposed to destroy him. Then afterwards He sent Judges, from time to time, to rescue them from their enemies; and Prophets also, to tell them of their duty, and to call them back from their sinful ways. But most of these Messengers met with the same reception. Though they were God's servants, they were treated with scorn. They had "trial of cruel mockings and scourgings, yea moreover of bonds and imprisonment. They were stoned, they were sawn asunder, were tempted, were slain with the sword." We read of Saul killing fourscore and five Priests in one day. We find the Prophet Elijah exclaiming, "The children of Israel have forsaken thy covenant, thrown down thine altars; and I, even I only, am left, and they seek my life to take it away." Jeremiah was cast into prison by order of King Zedekiah, for faithfully declaring the truth of God. Zechariah was stoned. And Isaiah is supposed to have been put to a cruel death by King Manasseh. You remember too our Lord's lamentation over the wicked inhabitants of Jerusalem—"O Jerusalem, Jerusalem, which killest the Prophets, and stonest them that are sent unto thee."

Thus then the treatment of the servants, by those wicked Husbandmen in the Parable, exactly described the treatment of the Prophets and other Messengers of God, by the very Jews in whose hearing it was spoken.

But this was not all. Their sin was even graver and deeper than this. "God, who at sundry times and in divers manners," had spoken "in time past unto the fathers by the prophets," was now speaking to them "by his Son." And how had they received Him? However they might have treated the inferior

Messengers, one might have expected that they would at all events reverence God's Son. But no: "He came unto his own, and his own received him not." He came to save the lost sheep of the house of Israel; but they rejected Him, and at length put Him to death as a malefactor. They dealt with Him, just as the men in the Parable dealt with their Master's Son—"This is the heir; come let us kill him." "Crucify him, crucify him."

They could not, they would not, "see any beauty in him, that they should desire him." When they beheld His miracles, they accused Him of being in league with the Evil One. When they heard His words of love and mercy, they stopped their ears, and hardened their hearts, against Him. When He spoke of being equal with God, they charged Him with blasphemy. Even His very lowliness offended them. They persecuted Him; they falsely accused Him; they seized Him; they scourged Him, and spat upon Him. And to such a height did their malice rise, that they never rested till they had shed His blood.

Such was the conduct of the unbelieving Jews; and to them did the Parable specially point. Here was the Master's Son, His only Son, His well-beloved, whom they took and killed, and cast out of the vineyard.

But was the Parable spoken for the Jews only? As we read it, do *we* feel altogether guiltless? Is *our* conscience so entirely clear, that we can say, That Parable has no word of conviction for *us?* Ah, has there not been a time, when we have lightly esteemed God's servants, when we have scorned their message, and turned away from it with indifference? There has probably been no violence on our part. These are not the days of outward violence. But still there has perhaps been in our hearts something of the same enmity, that there was in the hearts of the Jews.

But, it may be, we have gone further. Perhaps we have *taken part* with those who crucified Jesus. Can this be possible? you will ask. Yes, for although we lived not in the days of Herod and Pontius Pilate, yet we may have joined the betrayers and crucifiers of our Lord. If we have the same "evil heart of unbelief" which they had—if we have disobeyed Christ, as they did—then we are partakers of their sin. St. Paul speaks of some in his day "crucifying the Son of God afresh, and putting him to an open shame." And many do so now. Every sin men commit, be it great or small, be it outward or secret, is tearing open afresh the Saviour's wounds—it is adding to His pains and sufferings—it is lifting as it were an arm to smite Him.

It appears that Jesus, having finished the Parable, put a question to His Jewish hearers which made them pronounce their own condemnation. The question was this—"When the lord therefore of the vineyard cometh, what will he do unto those husbandmen?" He puts it to them, and invites them to pronounce their own verdict. And see what their answer was—"They say unto him, He will miserably destroy those wicked men, and will let out his vineyard unto other husbandmen, which shall render him the fruits in their seasons."

This was just the answer that our Lord wished. He wanted them to acknowledge how justly they themselves deserved to be cast off. And they did so most fully, though without intending it.

And now, in order to bring the matter still more home to them, He refers them to a verse in the Psalms, which they must often have read. "Jesus saith unto them, Did ye never read in the Scriptures, The stone which the builders rejected the same is become the head of the corner?"

That stone was Himself. They, the great Builders, were now rejecting Him—putting Him aside. But, in spite of their rejection, He would soon be exalted as the Head Corner Stone of the Building. Or, to go back to the Parable, *they* were the wicked Husbandmen, who rejected and slew their Master's Son. But the murdered Heir will one day take vengeance on His unthankful servants, and punish them for their sin.

Our Lord goes on to speak very plainly to them—"Therefore I say unto you, The kingdom of God shall be taken from you, and given to a nation bringing forth the fruits thereof." And He adds a most solemn warning—"Whosoever shall fall on this stone shall be broken; but on whomsoever it shall fall, it will grind him to powder."

These are awful words. All careless and

unbelieving sinners fall, as it were, on this Stone. They reject the truths of the gospel. They are blind, and stumble at them. And what will be the consequence? Much the same as if anyone were to stumble against the corner-stone of a building. They would not injure the stone by doing so; but they would greatly injure themselves. Thus the Prophet Isaiah, in chap. viii, speaking of the Lord of Hosts, says, "He shall be for a sanctuary; but for a stone of stumbling, and for a rock of offence to both the houses of Israel. And many among them shall stumble, and fall, and be broken, and be snared, and be taken."

Again, are there not some who go still further, and dare actually to oppose Christ, as the Jews did? On such the stone will "fall, and grind them to powder." The wrath of God will one day come down upon them; and they will be miserably destroyed, and will perish for ever.

It is thought by some, that Jesus alluded here to the custom of stoning malefactors. In such cases "a scaffold was erected twice the height of the person to be stoned. Standing on it, he was violently struck off by one of the witnesses. If he died by the blow and the fall, nothing further was done. But if not, a heavy stone was thrown down on him, which at once killed him." So with Jesus—the despised, the crucified one—on whom His enemies fell with such cruel malice and fury—He will one day fall upon them, and crush them for ever.

And now we have examined this Parable, and seen its meaning, and also the words which Jesus spoke at the conclusion of it.

Oh that we may never be ranged either among the opposers, or among the rejecters, of Christ! But may we believe on Him with all our hearts, and so may He be unspeakably precious in our eyes!

THE MARRIAGE SUPPER.

Matt. xxii. 1—14.

"And Jesus answered and spake unto them again by parables, and said, The kingdom of heaven is like unto a certain king, which made a marriage for his son, and sent forth his servants to call them that were bidden to the wedding: and they would not come. Again, he sent forth other servants, saying, Tell them which are bidden, Behold, I have prepared my dinner: my oxen and my fatlings are killed, and all things are ready: come unto the marriage. But they made light of it, and went their ways, one to his farm, another to his merchandise: and the remnant took his servants, and entreated them spitefully, and slew them. But when the king heard thereof, he was wroth: and he sent forth his armies, and destroyed those murderers, and burned up their city. Then saith he to his servants, The wedding is ready, but they which were bidden were not worthy. Go ye therefore into the highways, and as many as ye shall find, bid to the marriage. So those servants went out into the highways, and gathered together all as many as they found, both bad and good: and the wedding was furnished with guests. And when the king came in to see the guests, he saw there a man which had not on a wedding garment: and he saith unto him, Friend, how camest thou in hither not having a wedding garment? And he was speechless. Then said the king to the servants, Bind him hand and foot, and take him away, and cast him into outer darkness; there shall be weeping and gnashing of teeth. For many are called, but few are chosen."

(See also Luke xiv. 16—24.)

You remember that in one of the other Parables, namely the Parable of the Labourers in the Vineyard, our Lord concluded by saying, "For many be called, but few chosen." And here again, Jesus closes the Parable before us with the same words, " For many are called, but few are chosen."

There can be no doubt then as to the main truth, which the Saviour wished to teach by the Parable. His object was to show that His gospel call was to all; but that only a few would accept it, so as to be saved by it.

Let us see how He puts this before us. He bids us picture to ourselves a Marriage Feast. It is a Royal Marriage. " A certain king made a marriage for his son." Having given a sort of general invitation to his friends and acquaintance, as the wedding-day drew near, he sent out his summons to call them together. But they heeded not his kind message: they would not come. He invites them yet again, saying, "Tell them which are bidden, Behold I have prepared my dinner. My oxen and my fatlings are killed, and all things are ready: come unto the marriage." Still they refused, not for any particular reason; but simply because they had other matters to think about. "They made light of it, and went their ways, one to his farm, and another to his merchandise." Most of them, it seems, turned away from sheer carelessness. But some few went so far as to abuse and illtreat the king's messengers.

Now, when this reached the king's ears, he was exceedingly wroth at their conduct—to think that his messages should be thus scorned, and his messengers thus abused! He therefore gathers his army, punishes the offenders, and destroys the city in which they dwelt.

Let us see what Jesus meant by this part

of the Parable. He meant, I think, to shew that God, in the riches of His mercy, had provided salvation for His people—a full and plenteous salvation for all who would accept it. This is often compared to a Feast. Thus David says, in Ps. xxxvi., " How excellent is thy lovingkindness, O God! therefore the children of men put their trust under the shadow of thy wings. They shall be abundantly *satisfied with the fatness* of thy house." In Prov. ix., Solomon says, concerning wisdom, She hath " builded her house; she hath hewn out her seven pillars. She hath killed her beasts; she hath *mingled her wine; she hath also furnished her table.* She crieth . . . Come, eat of my bread, and drink of the wine which I have mingled." Isaiah, speaking of the Gospel, declares, " In this mountain shall the Lord of hosts make unto all people *a feast of fat things,* a feast of wines on the lees, a feast of fat things full of marrow, of wines on the lees well refined."

And is not the Gospel indeed *a Feast* to those who have hearts to receive it? Does not God thus " satisfy the longing soul, and fill the hungry soul with goodness"? Truly it is a Marriage Feast, tasted here on earth, but fully and completely enjoyed in heaven.

Then, the sending out of the Invitations to this Feast signifies the manner in which God calls men by His ministers, inviting them to believe the gospel, and to accept the salvation which He has so graciously provided.

Now, who were *the first persons* to whom Jesus offered salvation? To whom did He first go Himself, and afterwards send His messengers? It was to *the Jews*. They were His own people, His beloved friends, those who were nearest to His heart. " Come unto me," He said, " and I will give you rest." But they would not come. They made light of it. They cared more for the things of this world than for the things of heaven. They were more concerned about their forms and observances, about their farms and their merchandise, than about their souls.

And mark how close these words in the Parable came to their case. When they had rejected their Lord's message, then what followed? They were rejected themselves. The Roman army came against them, and their city Jerusalem was taken and destroyed. See how exactly the Parable describes this, though spoken forty years before—" When the king heard thereof, he was wroth; and he sent forth his armies, and destroyed those murderers, and burned up their city."

But let us go on with the Parable. The King, having prepared his Feast, and sent out his invitations, is treated with contempt, as we have seen, by the persons invited. But still he goes on inviting. He turns away from those who will not come, and sends his message to another class—"Then saith he to his servants, The wedding is ready, but they which were bidden were not worthy. Go ye therefore into the highways, and as many as ye shall find bid to the marriage." He enlarges his invitations. He calls, not merely his Friends and Acquaintances, but others also to the wedding—those who were less favoured—who were not so near to him— all, as many as could be found, he bids to the wedding feast.

This clearly describes God's call to the Gentiles, when the Jews refused to accept His salvation. The Jews were His immediate friends, His people, the sheep of His pasture. But the Gentiles (that is, all the rest) had hitherto been shut out from all religious privileges. They were afar off. They were "strangers and foreigners." After our Lord's ascension however, the gospel door was thrown open to receive them also. They might now enter in, and be saved.

This was a truth most hateful to Jewish ears —"that the Gentiles should be fellow-heirs, and of the same body, and partakers of God's promise in Christ by the gospel." For a while the Apostles themselves were slow to act upon it. But at length they saw that it was the will of God, and they obeyed. Hence we find Philip leaving the country of Judæa, and "going down to the city of Samaria, and preaching Christ unto them." Peter, again, baptized the Gentile Cornelius and his company. And Paul declared unto the men of Athens how God now "commandeth *all* men *everywhere* to repent."

But what is meant by the words "both bad and good," in ver. 10—"So those servants went out into the highways, and gathered together all, as many as they found, *both bad and good;* and the wedding was furnished with guests"?

When it is said that God's servants gather in the *bad*, as well as the *good*, I suppose those are meant who were *once* bad—who have nothing good in themselves to recommend them, but a feeling of their great need. So it was with the Corinthians; for St. Paul says of them, "Such were some of you; but ye are washed, but ye are sanctified, but ye are justified in the name of the Lord Jesus, and by the Spirit of our God." Thus an old writer, speaking of the Church, says, "Christ loved her, when she was *foul*, that He might make her *fair*."

What a mercy it is, Brethren, that the gospel is for *all*—for Gentiles, as well as Jews—for Publicans and Sinners, as well as for Pharisees—for those who have gone astray, as well as for those who have outwardly kept the strait path. It is for everyone who is content to lay aside his own righteousness, and accept the salvation of Christ— for everyone who is willing to part with sin, and walk in the ways of holiness. God's direction to His servants is, "Go ye therefore into the highways, and as many as ye shall find bid to the marriage." His invitation is,

"Ho, everyone that thirsteth, come ye to the waters; and he that hath no money; come ye, buy and eat; yea, come, buy wine and milk without money and without price."

And how glorious is the thought that hundreds and thousands have come to Christ, and found mercy! They have come from the East and from the West, from the North and from the South, and joined themselves to the Lord. And now the wedding table is furnished, as it were, with guests.

But let us pause for a moment, and bear in mind our Lord's words (verse 14)—"Many are called, but few chosen." Many who now enjoy gospel privileges, will never sit down with Christ in His kingdom. Many who are members of His Church on earth will never reach His Church above. This is further shewn by the closing portion of the Parable.

The King is represented as going into his supper room to see his guests. There is a goodly company gathered. But they are not all such guests as he would approve of. It is true, they were all invited. But as his eye passes from one to another, he sees here and there a man not clad in the Wedding Dress which was required. Addressing one, he says, "Friend, how camest thou in hither, not having a wedding garment?" The man is conscience-stricken, and answers not a word. He feels that he is there without having arrayed himself in the proper attire of a guest.

And was it reasonable, you may ask, to expect that one who had been brought in from the highways should provide himself with a fit dress to sit down at the king's table? Yes, it was reasonable; for it was customary at great feasts of this kind not only to furnish provisions, but also a fit dress which every guest might put on. The person therefore in the Parable who was not clothed in the wedding robe was without excuse. He *might* have obtained it. There was a garment for him, and he had only to put it on.

Now, what are we to understand by this *robe*—this *wedding garment?* What is it intended to signify? It means, I think, just that preparation of heart, without which no man can enter heaven. We must "put on Christ." We must be "clothed with the garments of salvation." We must be covered with the robe of righteousness. And if we are not thus clothed, there will be no heaven for us.

Such is the teaching of this beautiful Parable. It teaches us that God has abundantly provided for our souls' hunger—that He invites all to partake of His gospel blessings; but that many refuse, and that, of those who seem to accept the invitation, there are some who will never enter in, not having the wedding garment—or in other words, not having "put on Christ."

Now let us try and apply this to ourselves.

Have we heartily accepted the Gospel Invitation?

Some, like the Jews of old, absolutely *rebel* against God's way of salvation. Their hearts are too proud to submit to the Saviour's yoke. They not only see no beauty in Him, but their hearts are filled with enmity against Him.

Others there are, who do not oppose; but they feel altogether *unconcerned* about the offer made to them. They "neglect" the "great salvation." Like certain of those in the Parable, they "make light of it." They have their farms or their merchandise to attend to, and this takes up all their time and their thoughts. But oh how sad—to have souls, and not to care for them—to have an eternity before us, and to let earthly things keep it out of our thoughts—to have a Saviour who has died for us, and not to be saying to Him, "Lord, save me!"

There are others again, who have had some earnest feelings, and have come to Christ as their only refuge. They know and feel that "there is none other name under heaven given among men whereby we must be saved." And yet they have but a very *feeble* grasp of salvation. They cannot say, "Christ is mine; eternal life is mine; heaven is mine." No, there is still a clinging to the world. Their hearts are not wholly given to Christ. They follow Him, but it is afar off.

How is it with *you?* Have you heartily— yes, *heartily*—accepted the Gospel invitation? Are you following the Lamb whithersoever He goeth?

Once more, when the King looks down from heaven, does He see us with the Wedding-garment on? Without *faith* it is impossible to please God—without *love* we are but as sounding brass or a tinkling cymbal—without *holiness* we cannot see the Lord—without *Christ*, in short, we are naked and destitute. It is a solemn thought that many, who *seem* to be right, will be found wanting in that great day. Ministers may not detect them. How can they? For this garment is worn not on the body, but on the heart. Their friends may imagine that all is well with them. They themselves may fancy that they are in the way of safety. And yet He—He who looks through every false covering—He whose eye pierces the very heart—He will one day say to them, "I never knew you. How camest thou in hither, not having the wedding garment? You have not the mark of my people. You are among the many called, but not among the few chosen."

Oh that you and I may not deceive ourselves! May our hearts beat true to Christ! May we enjoy His happy service now, and hereafter sit down together at the marriage supper of the Lamb in heaven!

THE FORGIVEN DEBTOR.

LUKE VII. 40—43.

"And Jesus answering said unto him, Simon, I have somewhat to say unto thee. And he saith, Master, say on. There was a certain creditor which had two debtors: the one owed five hundred pence, and the other fifty. And when they had nothing to pay, he frankly forgave them both. Tell me therefore, which of them will love him most? Simon answered and said, I suppose that he, to whom he forgave most. And he said unto him, Thou hast rightly judged."

THE circumstance which led to this short and simple Parable was this—Jesus, happening to be at Bethany, was invited to the house of one of the Pharisees, named Simon. This man had probably some kind feeling towards our Lord, or he would not have received Him into his house. Perhaps, like Nicodemus, he was an inquirer after the truth, and therefore was glad to welcome the Saviour under his roof.

Whilst they were sitting at table, a Woman enters, and shows by her eagerness that there is some weighty matter upon her mind. Simon, the master of the house, is filled with astonishment, for the woman is a notorious character, well known for her evil life to all who dwelt at Bethany.

She comes, bringing in her hand a box of sweet-smelling ointment. She approaches the Saviour, places herself at His feet, and bursts into a flood of tears. Ah, such tears they were as she had never shed before—tears of bitterest sorrow—tears which flowed from the fountain of a broken and contrite heart. The big drops fell upon our Lord's feet, and she wiped them off, as they trickled down, with her long flowing hair.

At this Jesus shows no surprise, and no indignation. He does not send her away, as Simon expected, and as Simon probably would have done himself—saying, "Touch me not. Come not into my presence. Depart from me, thou sinful one." No, such was not *His* spirit, who came to save the lost—the Friend of Publicans and Sinners. But He knew more than Simon knew. He knew all that woman's history, past and present, just as He knows ours. He knew what those tears meant. He knew that she, who had been so great a sinner, was now a true penitent. He knew that her heart, once so full of evil, was now yearning for better things—that she was a lost one, seeking mercy from Him who was ever ready to bestow it.

Not a word seems to have been spoken either by the Woman, or by our Lord. But presently Simon breaks the silence. He is full of indignation, and mutters to himself, "This man, if he were a prophet, would have known who and what manner of woman this is that toucheth him: for she is a sinner." He had hitherto looked upon Jesus as a great Prophet; but now he almost doubts it. If He were indeed a discerner of hearts, would He receive such an one? Here was something of the old Pharisee-spirit rising up in Simon. He had much yet to learn both concerning himself, and concerning the Saviour. He had to learn the greatness of his own sins, and the wonders of that love of Christ which could reach down to the very worst of sinners.

Now, our Lord not only knew who this

woman was, and could read her whole character at a glance; but He also knew what was passing in Simon's mind. And this it was that made Him speak the Parable of the Two Debtors.

You see, the Woman during the last few minutes had given proof of her penitence, and also of her love to the Saviour. Her heart was drawn towards Him. And there she stood at His feet, anxious to hear from His lips some word of kindness and of mercy. Simon was for sending her away. But Jesus seemed to say, "Suffer her to come unto me, and forbid her not, for such penitents are welcome, such loving hearts are very dear to me."

And now for the Parable. There were two Debtors. One owed a much larger sum than the other—ten times as much. And neither of them had a farthing to pay the debt with. They were penniless. But the Creditor, the person to whom they owed the money, was a kind man; and instead of thrusting them into prison, forgave both of them their whole debt.

It is left to us to picture to ourselves what must have been the joy of these two men, when they found themselves thus free. We are not told anything about their gratitude or their happiness; but we may be quite sure that their hearts must have leapt for joy. Indeed our Lord leaves it to Simon to say, which of the two would naturally love his kind Benefactor the most. He takes it for granted that *both* would return love for such great kindness; but whose heart, He asks, would be *fullest?* Simon at once answers, and that rightly, "I suppose he to whom he forgave most."

No one can for a moment be at any loss to discover our Lord's meaning in this Parable. He Himself, as God, is the Great Creditor, and we are His Debtors—some owing fifty, and some five hundred, pence; but all owing Him something, and, what is more, unable to pay our debt.

These debts of ours, how great they are! We brought them with us into the world; and they have been gathering in amount ever since. Who among us can say how much we owe to our heavenly Father? There is not a day, nor an hour, when we have not incurred some fresh debt. And are there not some, who have gone on so recklessly, that their whole lives have been, as it were, one great transgression—one enormous debt. And yet this has not disturbed them, or made them uneasy. There was a time when their conscience smarted a little; but it soon grew callous, and sin became their daily habit; they could not live without it.

Oh, why did not the Lord seize them, and thrust them into His everlasting prison-house? Why did He not lay bare His arm, and smite them to the ground? He could have done so. Like a stern Creditor, He could have said, "Pay me that thou owest." He could have entered into judgment with them at once, and inflicted upon them the penalty they deserved.

But no. Mercy rejoiceth over judgment. He bears long with His guilty ones. He would not that any should perish, but that all should come to repentance. He says, "Deliver him from going down to the pit: I have found a ransom." He comes to the sinner, and whispers to him, "I, even I, am he that blotteth out thy transgressions, for

L

mine own sake." Yes, there is forgiveness with God. He loves to pardon. Think of Him sending His beloved Son to suffer in the sinner's stead—to pay our great and pressing debt. And then tell me, if we have not to do with one who is full of mercy, " who passeth by the transgression of the remnant of his heritage." *He* is that Creditor in the Parable, who is ever ready frankly to forgive our debts, if only we feel them grievous to us, and long to be released from them.

There is a sentence in the Apostles' Creed which is very full of comfort. I daresay we have repeated that sentence thousands of times, without feeling its preciousness. It is this—" I believe in the forgiveness of sins."

We are told that this short sentence brought much peace to the mind of Luther, when he was seeking the way of salvation. One day, when he was in great distress of mind, crying out, " O my sins, my sins!" a venerable old monk entered his cell, and Luther opened his heart to him. The old man scarcely knew the way of salvation himself; but he was often in the habit of repeating the Belief, and found much consolation in it for his own soul. So he repeated to Luther the words, "I believe in the forgiveness of sins." And those simple words, uttered at that moment, gave unspeakable consolation to Luther's mind. And from that hour light sprang up in his rejoicing heart.

And so it will be with us, if we can realize that blessed truth. For how does the forgiven debtor, the pardoned sinner, feel? Will not his gratitude be in proportion to the load which has been taken off his mind? Will not he, who has been forgiven much, love much?

Let the Woman in Simon's house answer the question. She came into our Lord's presence with a heavy load of sin upon her. She had lately felt its burden too heavy for her to bear. She had heard of Jesus. She had perhaps listened to His words. She knew Him to be the Saviour of the lost. She had faith to believe in His power and willingness to pardon her. She came to Him weary and heavy-laden, fully persuaded that He could give her rest. A feeling of love had already sprung up within her soul. And now, though He spoke not, His kind and gracious manner towards her filled her with confidence that she was indeed accepted.

Oh how thankful she felt when she stood before the Lord! Her tears were tears of penitence; but they were also tears of gratitude and love. Her sins came all before her— the sins of her youth, and of her later years— things that she had left undone, and things that she had done amiss—sins committed in the open day, and sins which had been concealed from the eye of her fellow-men—sins which perhaps the world might think little of, but which she knew to be sins in God's sight. Ah, these sins all crowded before her; and she felt herself to be guilty indeed. But then a ray of pardoning mercy burst, as it were, from the Sun of Righteousness, from the Saviour Himself. And all she further desired was to hear one little sentence from His lips—"Thy sins be forgiven thee." She already loved much, and felt anxious to give her pardoned life to Him who had given Himself for her.

I know not which is the most blessed and encouraging, the Parable, or the History which led to it. We may well thank God for both, and pray that we, like the Debtor who owed five hundred pence, and like the Woman in Simon's house, may know the comfort of a free forgiveness, and may be filled with love to Him who has loosed us from our debt.

Have you ever felt the weight of sin? It is possible you *may* not have felt it. It is possible you may *never* feel it. But there *is* a debt against us; and it is recorded in heaven. There it is, though we may not know it. Yes, and we must pay this debt, or perish. *We* must pay it, or another must pay it *for us.* Ah, has *He* not paid it, that gracious Saviour, that bleeding Lamb of God, who taketh away the sins of the world? The debt *is* paid to the uttermost farthing. Nothing remains of it. All is atoned for. "The blood of Jesus Christ cleanseth us from all sin." And what He waits for is to see us thankfully accept it. The words are already on His lips, "Thy sins be forgiven thee: go in peace."

Again, do you love your Saviour? *How much* do you love Him? Is it only *a little?* Alas, how small and feeble our love is! It is too apt to be a forced love—not the love that springs from a full heart.

The religion of many consists in a dry, dull round of duty. They serve God, because they are *obliged* to serve Him. It is a kind of prison labour with them—work which they feel they *must* do. But this should not be the case. We should rather say, "I *love* the service of my God. It is my delight, my enjoyment. Like the happy Bird, I fly at liberty on the wings of love to do His blessed will."

. What a difference there is between the Stream that creeps along in its dull, sluggish course, sometimes full, and sometimes almost dry—and the foaming Torrent that rushes forth, leaps over stones and rocks, and carries all before it! Which does our love most resemble? The trickling Stream, which is often dried up by the summer sun, and which at best flows but slowly along its track—or the joyous, bounding Torrent, which "rejoiceth as a strong man to run a race"?

Or again, what a difference there is between an artificial Flower, which looks gay for a moment, but grows dingy and faded as soon as the paint wears off—and those beautiful Flowers of Nature, which are ever fresh and lovely, and fill the air with their fragrance! Which does our love resemble? Is it only put on? Is it a mere imitation? Or is there a healthy bloom about it, which shows that it has a living root, and that it is a plant of God's own planting?

He that has had much forgiven loves much. Then, are we to conclude that to be true disciples we must needs have been great sinners? Is it an advantage to have committed multiplied transgressions? Are we to suppose that the wider a person has wandered from God, the nearer (if he has been brought back at all) he will live to Him afterwards—the more sin, the more love? Shall we say that to have sinned but little—to have been kept from gross offences—instead of being a blessing and a mercy, and a matter of thankfulness, may prove a hindrance to any strong, deep feeling of love to the Saviour?

No, it cannot be so. It is those who *feel* their sins the most—they are *in their own sight* the greatest sinners; they know their debt to be not fifty merely, but five hundred, pence;

and they, like St. Paul, regard themselves as "the *chief* of sinners." Yes, these are the ones who love much. They are ready to say, "The love of Christ constraineth us; because we thus judge, that if one died for all, then were all dead: and that he died for all, that they which live should not henceforth live unto themselves, but unto him which died for them, and rose again."

Pray that God, by His Holy Spirit, may convince you of sin, show you to yourself, strip off the covering which makes you *seem* better than you are, and send you as a guilty one to Christ, that He may pardon you; and that, feeling how much you have been forgiven, and how large your debt is, which has been paid for you, you may look up, and say, "Whom have I in heaven but thee?" "Lord, thou knowest that I love thee!"

THE NEIGHBOURLY SAMARITAN.

Luke x. 30—37.

" A certain man went down from Jerusalem to Jericho, and fell among thieves, which stripped him of his raiment, and wounded him, and departed, leaving him half dead. And by chance there came down a certain priest that way : and when he saw him, he passed by on the other side. And likewise a Levite, when he was at the place, came and looked on him, and passed by on the other side. But a certain Samaritan, as he journeyed, came where he was : and when he saw him, he had compassion on him, and went to him, and bound up his wounds, pouring in oil and wine, and set him on his own beast, and brought him to an inn, and took care of him. And on the morrow when he departed, he took out two pence, and gave them to the host, and said unto him, Take care of him ; and whatsoever thou spendest more, when I come again, I will repay thee. Which now of these three, thinkest thou, was neighbour unto him that fell among the thieves? And he said, He that shewed mercy on him. Then said Jesus unto him, Go, and do thou likewise."

WE will deal with this Parable as we have done with some of the others, and try if we can find out, in the first instance, *what led to its being spoken*.

There is no difficulty in discovering this in the present case; and indeed the whole Parable is so clear and simple, that it scarcely needs a word of explanation.

It appears from v. 25 that a certain Lawyer (that is, a man skilled in the writings of the Jewish law) stepped forward from among the crowd, and put what he considered a difficult question to our Lord. He freely acknowledged it to be our duty to love God with all our hearts, and our neighbour as ourselves. But he asks, *Who is my neighbour?*

Now, to this short question Jesus *might* have given an equally short answer. He might have replied, "*Every one* is thy neighbour." But instead of that, He takes the opportunity of shewing whom we ought to look upon as our neighbour, by a most beautiful and touching Parable. It was this—

A certain man had occasion to make a journey from Jerusalem to Jericho, which was a town about fifteen miles off. Now, in those days there were but few travellers, and probably no public conveyances. The road was through a rocky and mountainous country, and robberies were by no means unusual.

As the Traveller proceeds on his lonely way, he is attacked by Thieves, who strip him of everything, even of his very raiment; and then leave him by the road-side almost in a dying state.

Happy, for him, if the first passer-by proves to be a man of a kind and tender heart! Happy for him, if the first step he hears brings him the help which he so greatly needs! Let us see.

A person is passing along the road, and soon comes up to the very spot where the wounded man is lying. Does he stop and gladly offer him all the assistance in his power? One would expect it of him; for he turns out to be a Jewish Priest, a teacher of others, and one who ought to have known something of the law of kindness. But no; he just casts a glance at his suffering brother, and then passes onward on his way.

Presently another comes up. Ah, perhaps,

the poor man thinks, he will get more pity from him. This person is not exactly a Priest, but a *Levite*, a kind of helper to the Priests. And how does *he* act? He stops for a minute, gazes upon the helpless man, and proceeds on his way.

It is true the man was not *known* either to the Priest or to the Levite. But was he not a suffering fellow-creature, a brother in distress? If he had been an ox or an ass, fallen into a pit, ought they not to have helped him out? Neither of them however takes the trouble to do this. They had probably been worshipping at Jerusalem; but, whatever religious duties they had been performing there, they clearly "omitted now the weightier matters of the law, judgment, mercy, and faith." And they both had yet to learn what that meant, "I will have mercy, and not sacrifice."

But now another Traveller appears in the distance. It so happens that he is not only a *stranger*, but he belongs to *another nation*. He is a despised Samaritan. And we are told, that at that time there was a deadly quarrel between the Jews and the Samaritans. They had no dealings with one another.

From *him* then, at all events, the poor bleeding man can hardly expect any assistance. It is not likely that a Samaritan will shew much feeling for a Jew, one of his bitter enemies. And yet even *he* shall teach us a lesson of brotherly kindness. He does not stop to consider whether the wounded man is one of his own nation or not. He is helpless and in distress, and that is enough for him. He dismounts from the beast on which he is riding, sits down by his brother's side, speaks a few kind words to him; and then binds up his bleeding wounds, lifts him up upon his own beast, and takes him to the nearest Inn.

This is not all. The kind Samaritan, instead of going forward on his way, stops there for the night, to watch by the suffering stranger. And when he leaves him the next morning, he pulls out two pence, which was enough to pay for the night's lodging; and then charges the Innkeeper to see after him, promising himself to be answerable for any further expense that may be incurred.

This then was the Parable by which Jesus met the Lawyer's enquiry, *Who is my neigh-*

bour? And now, seeing perhaps that he was interested in the story, and struck by the lesson which it so plainly taught, He leaves it to him to give his own reply to the question—" Which now (the Saviour asks), which of these three, thinkest thou, was neighbour unto him that fell among the thieves? And he said, He that shewed mercy on him. Then said Jesus unto him, Go and do thou likewise." As much as to say, You enquire, " Who is my neighbour? " Learn that if you have a really Christian spirit you will feel that *every man*—be he a stranger, or an acquaintance—be he a foreigner, or a fellow-countryman—be he a friend, or a foe— *every man* is to you a neighbour, and you should act a neighbour's part towards him.

And now let not the Saviour's words be thrown away upon us. Let us " go and do likewise."

First, let us look upon *every one as our neighbour*. This is perhaps almost a new idea to you. It may be, you have hitherto thought that only those who happen to live *near you* are your neighbours—that only your acquaintance, or your friends, or those who have done you some act of kindness have any claim upon you—that you need not concern yourself about others. But this is not the gospel rule. The gospel bids us cast aside our selfishness. It bids us feel for our brethren, be interested about them, and be ever ready to help them. If any one suffers, it calls upon us to suffer with him, or if any one rejoices, to rejoice with him. A true Christian will not be cold, and hard, and suspicious; but he will remember that all are children of the same Father, are travellers through the same wilderness, and are invited to the same resting-place. Oh there is much to knit us to one another.

Of course we cannot feel towards all alike. There are ties which bind some more closely to us than others. There are the ties of kindred and friendship. We feel very near to those among whom we have been brought up. A real Christian too will especially love his brother Christians—those who are following Christ. Again, we are more closely drawn towards those who belong to the same Church as ourselves, who are members of the same

Christian Body. But still there is a love—a lesser love perhaps, but a real love—which we ought to feel towards *others*. We should be like the glorious Sun in the heavens, which shines upon all, and makes everyone feel its blessed, cheering rays. Yes, we should learn to look upon every fellow-creature, whoever he may be, as our *neighbour*.

But our kind feeling must shew itself by *acting*. If the Tree is good, it will bring forth fruit. Now, there are *many ways* in which we may shew kindness. There are many ways in which we may act the Samaritan's part.

Is any one *in distress?* Do not suppose you can do nothing for him. He may want money, and you have perhaps none to give him. He may want food, and you can barely supply your own family. But are these the *only* wants he has? Is this his *only* trouble? Perhaps he has wants which you can and may supply. The friendly countenance of a neighbour may cheer him. Kind, gentle, Christian words may soothe his aching heart. The mere feeling that some one cares for him may be like medicine to his soul.

Or is anyone *laid by from illness?* He is confined to his sick room. Wearisome days and lonely nights are appointed him. The hours perhaps drag heavily along. Here is an opportunity for you. In that cottage lies an afflicted Brother or Sister. Do you know it, and yet not so much as ask, if you can do anything for the sufferer? Will you, like the Priest or the Levite, pass by on the other side? Will you say, like Cain, "Am I my brother's keeper?" Ah, you may step in, and be useful. The visit of a Christian neighbour, however poor he may be, is often unspeakably welcome. It is "as cold water to a thirsty soul." It may cheer; it may encourage; it may soften; it may be as a balm to the wounded spirit; it may help on the way to heaven.

Or again, is there any one *ignorant or careless?* "Here is a case for a minister," you will say. But still, can *you* do nothing? Though you may not have much learning yourself, you may tell him the little that you know. You may persuade him to come to God's house, where he will hear more, and where he may learn what will be a great blessing to his soul. "Come thou with us," you can say, "and we will do thee good." Or, you may talk kindly to him; and he may open his mind to you, and tell you what keeps him back from God, when perhaps he would be half afraid to speak to his Clergyman.

Don't say, "I have no time for such neighbourly acts. I have other business to attend to. This is not my calling." The good Samaritan in the Parable had perhaps other business. Very likely it was important for him to arrive that night at Jericho. But he put all aside for the sake of the poor wounded Traveller. And see what *trouble* he took for him, though he was a perfect stranger. He stopped on his journey. He bound up his wounds. He set him on his own beast. He took him to the inn. He passed the night in nursing him; and took care that he was attended to after he left him.

But there is yet another class of persons, on whom our Christian kindness may be well spent. I mean *our Heathen Brethren*. They have the same wounded souls that we have, but no one to pour in oil and wine—no one to bind up their wounds. There they lie in their misery, as sheep without a shepherd. They are not our *countrymen*, you will perhaps say. Neither was the Traveller the Samaritan's fellow-countryman. We may not be able to go to them ourselves: but we may do as he did when he left the inn—we may give our money to those who are able and willing to go and help them.

Such are some of the many ways, in which we may act according to the teaching of this Parable, and follow the example of that good Samaritan. *We* may go and do likewise. Try to do so; and your life will become a useful and a happy one, and you will be doing some good in the world. You may be weak; but if you look up for God's strength, He will assuredly make you an instrument of much blessing.

I cannot conclude, without mentioning that there are some who see another and a still *deeper meaning* in this Parable. They see, in the conduct of the good Samaritan, a picture of our *blessed Lord Himself*—coming as He did to seek and to save the lost, binding up the broken-hearted, and giving rest to the weary and the wounded.

I do not think that this was *intended* by our Lord; but it *may* have been so. And at all events we know that no love was ever like His love, no pity like His pity; and no one ever did such great things for us as He has done. For not only did He stoop down to help us in our misery, but He Himself was "*wounded* for our transgressions, and bruised for our iniquities." He shed for us His own most precious blood, that we might live for ever! Oh amazing goodness! May it touch our hearts, and win us over to Him!

THE RICH FOOL.

Luke xii. 16—21.

"And he spake a parable unto them, saying, The ground of a certain rich man brought forth plentifully: and he thought within himself, saying, What shall I do, because I have no room where to bestow my fruits? And he said, This will I do: I will pull down my barns, and build greater: and there will I bestow all my fruits and my goods. And I will say to my soul, Soul, thou hast much goods laid up for many years; take thine ease, eat, drink, and be merry. But God said unto him, Thou fool, this night thy soul shall be required of thee: then whose shall those things be, which thou hast provided? So is he that layeth up treasure for himself, and is not rich toward God."

We have only to look back to the thirteenth verse, and we shall at once see what gave rise to the Parable now before us.

Our Lord had been addressing a considerable crowd of people; and one of the company steps forward, and asks Him to settle a certain family difference, which seems to have taken up much of the man's thoughts—" Master, speak to my brother, that he divide the inheritance with me." Jesus at once refuses this request; " Man, who made me a judge or a divider over you ? " As much as to say, " I have other work to do, besides settling mere worldly disputes; and there are often matters for *you* to think of, besides the uncertain possessions of this world."

And then this conversation leads our Saviour to utter the Parable before us—a Parable which shews us how entirely any one may be drawn away by feelings of covetousness and worldly-mindedness.

This is one of the many instances in which we find our Lord seizing a passing opportunity, and turning it to good account—taking advantage of a wrong request which was made to Him, to give some very seasonable instruction to His hearers.

His Text was *Covetousness*, or a grasping spirit : and upon that Text, as it were, He preaches to them in the form of a Parable.

He bids us picture to ourselves the case of a Farmer, with whom things are going well.

"The ground of a certain rich man," He says, "brought forth plentifully." His land produced an unusual crop, so that his barns and granaries were not large enough to contain his stores. What is he to do? Why, he naturally resolves to pull them down, and build greater. But he does not rest there. His prosperity carries him completely away; and he begins to fancy that his possessions will last for ever. He says to himself, "Soul, thou hast much goods laid up for many years: take thine ease, eat, drink, and be merry."

But suddenly, whilst he is laying out his plans for the worldly happiness before him, God puts in a word to show him the utter folly of his dreams. He whispers to him, "Thou fool, this night thy soul shall be required of thee." Thus in a moment all his fond expectations are cut off. The sentence goes forth. He is summoned, with only a few hours' warning, to stand before God, and to give up his account.

Such is the Parable. By it we are taught the folly of those who think only of laying up their stores here, but have no treasure in heaven.

Let us try and apply the Parable to ourselves.

There is *a danger in prosperity*. We all like to be prosperous. If you have a field or a garden, you like it to bring forth plentifully. You would rejoice if your yearly income, or your weekly wages, might be a little higher. Yes, we all like prosperity. But there is a danger in it. I have read of a clergyman, who once called on a member of his congregation: and after the usual salutation he thus addressed him—" I understand you are very dangerously situated." The other answered with much surprise, " I was not aware of it." The clergyman then said, " I thought it was probable you were not, and therefore I called on you. I hear, you are getting rich. Take care, for it is the road by which Satan leads thousands to destruction." This was spoken with so much earnestness, that the prosperous man was greatly struck by it.

Yes, there is danger in prosperity. It sets us in slippery places. There is many a one who does very well, as long as he is a little down. But a fortunate turn comes in his affairs. He grows rich; and forthwith he is thrown off his balance. The world has now many more charms for him. He clings to it with eagerness. He has got money; but he is by no means satisfied with it; he wants more. Perhaps he once thought about his soul; but now other thoughts, worldly thoughts, crowd in. Once he felt a delight in heavenly things: now his mind is full of the world, and Christ and heaven are thrust aside.

Is it not often so, when things go well with us? Have we not found that the day of adversity was much more favourable for religion, than the brighter day of prosperity? It is for this reason that our Church, like a watchful Mother, teaches us to pray, " In all times of our *wealth* (or wellbeing), good Lord, deliver us."

We may learn too from this Parable that *ungodly men sometimes prosper in the world.* David says, " I have seen the wicked in great prosperity, flourishing like a green bay tree." Prosperity is no sign of God's favour, nor is adversity any sign of His anger. He sometimes gives men their desire; but " sends leanness into their souls." It is better, far better, to be poor and godly, than to be rich and worldly. It is better to have a lack of this world's goods, with Christ in our hearts, and heaven in prospect, than to fare sumptuously every day, and to live without God in the world. "Better is little with the fear of the Lord, than great treasures and trouble therewith."

Another thing which we are reminded of here, and which we all so much need to be reminded of, is that *God's summons may come to us at any moment.*

The man in the Parable had no idea of death being near. This was the very last thing he thought of. He boasts not merely of to-morrow, but of years to come. He expects to "multiply his days as the sand." "To-morrow shall be as this day, and much more abundant." But the summons comes—"This night thy soul shall be required of thee." Like the king of Babylon, he is stopped short in the midst of his career, and told to prepare for death.

O thoughtless, careless one, how should you

feel, if such a summons were to come to you? And yet it *may* come. It has come as suddenly to many. It may come so to *you*. You may be called away in all your unreadiness—in the midst of your sin, your unbelief, your love of this world. You have neglected your soul, and that soul is required of you. You must stand before God just as you are, without Christ, without hope, with no meetness for heaven. Ah, there will be "no more sacrifice for sin," no fresh offers of mercy will be made to you. If the door of heaven is once closed against you, it will be closed for ever.

And are there not some who are neither thoughtless perhaps, nor careless; for their thoughts are often turned towards another world—but yet they are not ready to die? If an Angel were to come, and say to you, "This year thou shalt die," would it not startle you? Would it not disturb you in some of the plans you are forming? Would not one of your first feelings be, "I have not lived near enough to my God. I have not clung closely enough to my Saviour. I am not making religion 'the one thing needful.' I dare not live as I have been living, during this coming year—this last year—of my life."

Even a year would seem but a little span. But suppose the messenger were to say, "This *week*, or this *night*, thy soul shall be required of thee," should you receive the news calmly and without alarm? Could you say, "I know whom I have believed. My soul is safe for eternity. To me to live is Christ, and to die is gain. I desire to depart and to be with my Saviour"? Very few, I fear, are in this prepared and waiting state. And yet, as Christ's people, we *should* be ready. Like the captive Bird, we should be ever watching, the moment the cage door is unbarred, to fly away, and mount upwards to heaven.

Oh for more of this readiness—to be so weaned from all things here below—to have such a clear, firm hold of Christ—that death can never come too soon—that God's summons can never take us by surprise; but that we shall be always waiting for, and even longing for, our call to enter into the presence of our Lord!

But the great Lesson which Jesus teaches

us in this Parable is, that *we should "beware of covetousness."* A covetous, money-loving spirit soon grows upon us. How wise was the warning of the Psalmist, "If riches increase, set not your heart upon them." And Solomon says, " Labour not to be rich." We should guard against the first appearance of such a spirit. Oh, how it cramps and chills our love to God! How it weakens our faith, and deadens our affections! A grasping, money-loving man can never give himself heartily to God, can never ripen for heaven. No, his complaint must ever be, "My soul cleaveth unto the dust."

Our Lord in this Parable draws the curtain back, and lets us look into the inner chamber of a worldling's heart. It is anything but a happy picture: it is a very sad one. See him making provision for bodily gratification, but no provision whatever for the soul. Hear him reckoning up his riches, as if they were his own. He talks about "*my* fruits, and *my* goods."

What folly! For suddenly he discovers, to his great surprise, that they are not his; but the great Owner, from whom they came, and whose they are, requires them of him.

I am sure we all feel that this Parable is true to the life. And yet how is it that we are so eager to possess? How is it that we look with a longing eye upon the prosperous? The truth is, we *see* what a man has, and therefore we *envy* him. But if we could also see how little enjoyment he has of his possessions, we should oftener *pity* him.

It is here said that the man who trusts in riches is a "fool." He is a fool in God's eyes, and soon he will be a fool in his own eyes. The Lord seems to say to him, "Thou fool, thou art grasping a mere empty shadow. Thou art pressing to thy bosom a thorn. Thou art making for thyself golden weights, which will keep thee down to earth. Thou art rich, in men's estimation. 'Thou art increased with goods,' say they, 'and hast need of nothing'; but I, thy God, tell thee that thou art poor, miserably poor, as regards thy soul."

And now we have plainly seen where our *folly* lies. May we not also gather from our

Lord's teaching what is our *wisdom* also. It is to seek after *true* riches. There is a treasure, which may be laid up in heaven—a treasure which never fails—which neither moth nor rust doth corrupt, and which no thief can steal from us.

A writer, who lived more than a thousand years ago, tells us that we need not *lose* our riches, but *change their place.* He says:— "Suppose a friend should enter thy house, and should find that thou hadst lodged thy fruits on a damp floor. And suppose he knew the likelihood of those fruits to spoil; and should therefore give thee some such advice as this— 'Brother, thou art likely to lose the things which thou hast gathered with great labour. Thou hast placed them on a damp floor. In a few days they will corrupt.' You would inquire, 'What shall I do?' And he would answer, '*Raise them to a higher room.*' Now, you would listen to such advice, and no doubt instantly act upon it. Will you not, then, hearken to Christ, who advises you to *raise your treasure from earth to heaven?*"

How wise it would have been of that worldly-minded man in the Parable, if, instead of saying, "I will pull down my barns, and build greater," he had said, "I will provide myself bags which wax not old, a treasure in the heavens that faileth not,"—if he had spent his riches in doing good—if he had laid them out in providing for his poorer brethren, and so lent them, as it were, to the Lord—if he had made the bosoms of the needy his barns (barns which would last for ever)—then he would have been rich in God's sight. And again, if he had felt the utter uncertainty of all here, and had sought in earnest the salvation of his never-dying soul, then all would have been well with him.

We may all of us lay up a treasure in heaven. We may all be growing rich for eternity. How—where—is this treasure to be obtained? Christ says, "Buy of *me* gold tried in the fire, that thou mayest be rich." Christ can make the poorest of us wealthy. He Himself is our treasure, the Pearl of great price. If we possess Him, we possess all. If we can say, "Christ is mine," we can say, "All is mine; Pardon is mine; Peace is mine; Heaven is mine; God is my God."

"Go," said the Saviour to the rich young

man, who came to Him—" Go, and sell that thou hast, and thou shalt have treasure in heaven, and come and follow me." Go, dear Friend, say I—Go, and part to-day with your sins, with your love of the world. Part with the poor, thread-bare cloak of your own righteousness, which you have perhaps worn so long, and wrapt so closely round you. Throw it off, and put on Christ, and accept Him as your portion. The world may despise you for doing so. The world may consider it folly. But blessed are those who are willing to "count all else but loss that they may win Christ, and be found in Him."

THE FRUITLESS FIG-TREE.

LUKE XIII. 6—9.

"He spake also this parable; A certain man had a fig tree planted in his vineyard; and he came and sought fruit thereon, and found none. Then said he unto the dresser of his vineyard, Behold, these three years I come seeking fruit on this fig tree, and find none: cut it down; why cumbereth it the ground? And he answering said unto him, Lord, let it alone this year also, till I shall dig about it, and dung it: and if it bear fruit, well: and if not, then after that thou shalt cut it down."

IF we look at the five first verses of the chapter, we shall see what led to the Parable before us. Some persons came to tell our Lord of a judgment which had just fallen on certain Galileans. And they told it in such a way as if they felt that these Galileans must have been very great sinners, or they would not thus have suffered. This feeling was a wrong one; and Jesus reproves it, adding this warning, "I tell you, Nay; but except ye repent, ye shall all likewise perish." This it was which led to the Parable which follows, in which our Lord urges the necessity of repentance, and of bringing forth fruit to God.

Our eye is at once directed to a Fig-tree. "A certain man had a fig-tree." And this was not a neglected or uncared-for tree, which grew by the roadside, as was often the case in Judæa. But it was planted in the choicest place which the owner could select for it, namely, in his Vineyard. This was usually a favoured spot on the Farm, where the soil was rich, and the ground well tilled. Here then he plants his Fig-tree, hoping, no doubt, and expecting, that it would be a productive tree, and one that would amply repay his care.

In the summer time he comes, and seeks for fruit; but there is none to be seen. There are *leaves* enough, but no *figs*. How is this? There has been no neglect. The tree has been cared for. The soil is good. There is no appearance of any one having come and stript it. No; the tree *itself* is in fault. It is worthless and barren. It has ill repaid all "the Dresser's" care.

The Owner at once proposes to cut it down, as a useless cumberer of the ground. It was taking up room that might be better filled. There is a little pause however; for the Dresser of the vineyard (that is, the person who looks after it) pleads for the Tree, and entreats that it may be left standing yet another twelve months. And then, he says, if it is found to bear fruit, all will be well; and if not, then it must come down. So the tree was left; but we are not told how it fared.

Now, that Fig-tree describes the Jew in former days, and the Christian in these days; for what the Jew was once, we are now. We Christians are specially blest and favoured by God, cared for, and enjoying every spiritual advantage. We are members of God's Church.

Many of our fellow-creatures have not the

same religious blessings as we have. They are living perhaps in some heathen country, like neglected trees by the wayside, with none to feel a concern for them—growing wild, as it were, with no Dresser to cultivate them. Or their dwelling may be in a Christian land like ours; but in some overgrown and crowded city, where the gospel hardly reaches them, and no one is concerned about their souls.

How thankful should we be, if our lot is different from this—if, like the fig-tree in the vineyard, we have been thought of, cultivated, and watched over! But let me ask, when the great Owner comes year after year, does He find us as we ought to be, growing in grace, and rich in good works? Or does He find us barren and unfruitful—members of His Church, but worthless members—Christians in name, but not loving Christ, and not living as His true and believing people?

When we turn our thoughts back on the past day, or on the past year, is there not much, very much, to make us sad? How many things have we left undone, or done wrongly? What have our prayers been—our prayers in God's house, or our prayers at home? Alas, oftentimes a mere form. I remember reading of a Dream, in which an Angel was supposed to have mixed with a congregation of worshippers. There was a great noise—a great buzz of words, in that congregation. Many *seemed* to be worshipping God. But the Angel heard only a very few voices in that great crowd; for no voice reached *his* ear, but the voice of those who were really praying. There were many lips moving, and many words uttered; but it seemed to him as if only a very few were either praying or singing praises to God.

How has it been with us, when we have gone to the house of God? How has it been in our private chambers? Have mere sounds gone forth from our lips, or, if the Angel had been present, would he have heard real prayer from our hearts? Again, have we read our Bibles earnestly, thoughtfully, and prayerfully? Have we made any growth in the Christian life? Are we healthier, and riper, and holier than we were a year or two ago? Now, do not let this be a mere passing thought, but a deep and solemn inquiry, a matter for searching self-examination.

Like the Owner of the Fig-tree, God comes oftentimes, seeking fruit; and woe unto us, if, as it was in the Parable, He finds none. We may not be very bad in the eyes of our fellow-men; but still, if God finds us fruitless, showing no signs of spiritual life, giving no proof that our hearts are right with Him, then is it not reasonable that He should turn away from us in anger, and utterly forsake us?

You and I, dear Reader, profess to be Christians. We bear Christ's name. We are members of a religious Body. Ah, this will be of no use to us, unless we have grace in our hearts, and holiness in our lives— unless we are Christians in very deed. Better for us to have been heathens, or to have lived out of the reach of Christian ordinances. For then we might have pleaded lack of culture—we might have said, in our defence, "No man careth for my soul." But we cannot say this now. We dare not say it. We may not have been cared for as we ought perhaps; but still we have been cared for. Those who have been set as dressers of the vineyard may have been wanting on many points; but still they have dressed it. Salvation has been held out to us. We have heard of the Saviour's blood. We have been counselled—yea, intreated—to flee from the wrath to come. Then, if we are lost, *we* must bear the burden.

How fearful those words are, "Cut it down. Why cumbereth it the ground"? This is the sinner's sentence. The Fig-tree not only occupied the place, which might have been filled by another and a better tree, but it injured the land, drawing off nourishment from it without making any return. And so the sinner, who lives without God, is not only useless and unprofitable; but his bad life and his evil example are positively hurtful to all around him, and are a stumbling-block to others in the way of their salvation.

"Cut it down," says the Husbandman. "Cut him off; and let him perish," says God, when His patience has been long tried. And why has not this sentence gone out against you and me? Why are we still living—still allowed to hear the Gospel, and listen to a Saviour's gracious invitation? How is this?

We have most of us deserved to be cut off, and yet we are alive to-day, and within reach of mercy?

Ah, there has been a Pleader in our behalf. There is one who has said, "Let it alone this year also, till I shall dig about it, and dung it; and if it bear fruit, well; and if not, then after that thou shalt cut it down." He does not say, "Lord, let it never be cut down"— but "Lord, *not now.*" "Lord, do not remove the dresser, do not withhold the dew, do not pluck upthe tree *just yet.*"

Thank God, we may *all* be pleaders for one another; and we are assured that "the prayer of a righteous man availeth much." Abraham pleaded for Sodom, Gen. xviii. 23; Moses for Israel, Ex. xxxii. 11; Job for his children, Job xlii. 8; Samuel for his people, 1 Sam. xii. 23. And many a mercy has come to *us* perhaps, through the prayer of some Christian brother.

But Jesus is the *Great Pleader*. It may be, He has pleaded for us again and again; and it is perhaps owing to His intercession that we are spared to this day. He who "bare the sin of many," as the Prophet says, "and made intercession for the transgressors"—He who prayed as He hung upon the cross, "Father, forgive them"—He it is who maketh intercession for us before the throne of God; and the hand of justice has been stayed.

Observe too *the various ways in which the Lord deals* with us, and *the object He has in view.*

The object for which the Fig-tree was *planted,* and cared for, was that it should bear fruit. And for this object it is now *spared*—"If it bear fruit, well; and if not, then after that thou shalt cut it down." And such is the great end for which God shews His forbearance towards us—it is that we may become fruit-bearing Christians; "Herein is my Father glorified, that ye bear much fruit." Leaves will not satisfy Him—a mere profession of religion. Blossoms will not satisfy Him— beginning well, and promising fair. There must be *fruit.*

And to make the Tree fruitful, what does the Dresser do? He digs about it, and dungs it; he breaks up the earth that is round it, and manures it, in order to give it more vigour. And so does God deal with us. Sometimes He cuts and wounds us, as it were. At other times He breaks up, and removes, the things around us—our friends, our comforts, our money. He strips us, and lays us bare. But all in mercy, if that by any means He may save our souls.

But the great truth which shines forth like a bright star in this Parable is *the wonderful Forbearance of God*.

How marvellous it is that, although we have been provoking God every day, He has been every day bearing with us. Although we have been wearying Him by our iniquities, He has been unwearied in His mercy towards us. Although we have sinned against Him time after time, He has not crushed us. Is not this a proof of God's great kindness; and should not our hearts be melted by it? Well may the Apostle ask us, " Despisest thou the riches of his goodness, and forbearance, and long-suffering; not knowing that the goodness of God leadeth thee to repentance"? When St. Paul thought of those days, during which he so deeply grieved his Saviour, "breathing out threatenings and slaughter against the disciples of the Lord," his heart must have glowed with thankfulness at the patience which had been shewn towards him—"Howbeit I obtained mercy, that in me first Jesus Christ might shew forth all longsuffering." And shall not *we*, if at least we know anything of ourselves, cry out, "Who is a God like unto thee, that pardoneth iniquity, and passeth by the transgression of the remnant of his heritage? He retaineth not his anger for ever; because he delighteth in mercy."

God is usually very slow to punish. And often does He wait and wait, before His wrath comes down upon us. Just as the axe is often laid down at the root of the tree, before the Woodman lifts his arm to cleave it, so does God pause, before He strikes the threatened blow. Before the flood, He gave a hundred and twenty years of warning; as St. Peter says, "The longsuffering of God *waited* in the days of Noah." It was not until "the iniquity of the Amorites was *full*," that the sentence which had long been pronounced against them was carried into effect.

Jesus, when on earth, plainly declared that Jerusalem, the unbelieving city, should be destroyed; but the Lord *waited* forty years before His judgments were poured upon it. And St. Peter tells us, that the coming of the great day of Christ is put off through the forbearance of God towards sinners—" The Lord is not slack concerning his promise, as some men count slackness; but is longsuffering to usward, not willing that any should perish."

Long does He forbear to bring the evil. He *threatens*, in the hope that He may not be forced to *inflict* what He threatens. He *speaks* once, yea twice, that he may not *strike*. He *shews* the rod, before He *uses* it. Drops come down from the dark thunder-cloud, before "wrath is poured out to the uttermost."

And ought not God's longsuffering towards us to kindle within us a like feeling *towards one another?* Has He borne so much evil from us? Have we for years existed, as it were, upon His longsuffering? And shall we be harsh towards each other—be ready to notice every infirmity in our brother—and be unwilling to pass by a single fault, though God has seen so many in us? After having been forgiven the Ten Thousand talents, shall we take our fellow-servant by the throat for an Hundred pence?

Oh that we may bring forth much fruit, and especially the lovely fruit of patience, forbearance, and brotherly kindness! And when the Lord of the vineyard comes, may you and I be found "neither barren nor unfruitful"—that so "an entrance may be administered unto us abundantly into the everlasting kingdom of our Lord and Saviour Jesus Christ!"

THE HUMBLE GUEST EXALTED.

Luke xiv. 7—11.

"And he put forth a parable to those which were bidden, when he marked how they chose out the chief rooms; saying unto them, When thou art bidden of any man to a wedding, sit not down in the highest room; lest a more honourable man than thou be bidden of him; and he that bade thee and him come and say to thee, Give this man place; and thou begin with shame to take the lowest room. But when thou art bidden, go and sit down in the lowest room; that when he that bade thee cometh, he may say unto thee, Friend, go up higher: then shalt thou have worship in the presence of them that sit at meat with thee. For whosoever exalteth himself shall be abased; and he that humbleth himself shall be exalted.

THERE is *a Circumstance* here mentioned, which led our Lord to speak one of His Parables. Then, we have *the Parable itself*. And lastly *the Lesson* which the Parable was intended to teach us.

The *Circumstance* which occurred was this —Our Lord, being in the house of one of the Pharisees, whilst He was sitting with him and his friends at table, noticed some of the guests putting themselves forward, and choosing the highest seats. He determines to check this unseemly forwardness; and not only so, but to expose the secret feeling of pride which was at the root of it. And with this end in view, He speaks the Parable.

When you are invited to a Feast, He says, do not choose for yourself the foremost place, but rather take the lowest seat at the table. For there may chance to be present some of higher rank, and more deserving, than yourself. And then, if the Master of the feast should say to you, "Go down lower, and make way for this or that person," you will be filled with shame at being obliged to do so. But if, on the other hand, you choose for yourself a low place, the Master of the house may perhaps say to you, "Friend, come up higher" —"Take a more honourable seat." Then shall you have worship (that is, respect paid you) from those who are present.

Such is the Parable. Now, what was our Lord's meaning? He did not mean to teach us merely how to behave at table. The Parable has a much wider meaning. And lest we should miss it, Jesus tells us plainly, in the last verse, what that meaning is—" For whosoever exalteth himself shall be abased: and he that humbleth himself shall be exalted."

This Parable then is intended to teach us *Humility*—that God will bring down those who exalt themselves; and that, on the other hand, He will raise up those who are humble and lowly.

Pride is natural to us all. It is part of our evil nature. The Rich man is proud of his wealth, the Learned man of his wisdom. There is the pride of money, and the pride of rank. There is the pride of beauty, and the pride of dress. There is pride to be found among the great people in our towns, and pride too among the poorest in our villages. Pride is to be seen creeping in everywhere, even into the very house of God. Yes, we may trace its footsteps even in the Sanctuary. One person thinks of his fine clothes, whilst he is there. And another stays away altogether, because he cannot appear so well dressed as his neighbour. One person shuts himself into his pew, and grudges to make way for anyone who has not an actual right to sit with him. Another again refuses to come at all, because he cannot have what he considers his proper seat.

How sad it is that this hateful sin should so cleave to us! Men despise us for it; and what is far worse, God condemns us: it disfigures us in His sight.

But the worst of this Pride is that it keeps us from Christ. The Word of God tells us that we are sinners. Sin is one of the few things we may call our own. We need not go here or there to discover it. Here it is, in our hearts. And if you or I have any good hope of heaven, it is because we have found pardon for our sins—we have found Him who is the sinner's Friend.

We are told in the Bible that man is a sinner, and that Christ is the only Saviour. This is a truth so plainly set forth, that no one will deny it. We may read it in almost every part of God's Word; and if we look into our Prayer-book, we shall find it there also.

And yet numbers remain at a distance from Christ. Why is this? How shall we account for it? It is pride. People will acknowledge that Holy Scripture speaks of us as sinners. We know that the very prayers we offer up in God's house echo the same truth. But our hearts are oftentimes too proud to allow it *in our own case.* Christ is offered to us continually. He is constantly passing by, as it were, and saying to us, " Wilt thou be made whole?" He sees us to be poor, and blind, and naked; but we see it not ourselves. We will not own it. We will not come to Him, that we might have life.

Thank God, He does sometimes crush this pride of ours. His grace reaches our very hearts, and lays us low in the dust. When this is the case, all our fancied goodness is scattered to the winds. We feel that we are nothing, and that Christ is everything. . We are ready to exclaim with Job, " I have heard of thee by the hearing of the ear, but now mine eye seeth thee: wherefore I abhor myself, and repent in dust and ashes." .

Look again at these words of Christ now before us—" Whosoever exalteth himself shall be abased; and he that humbleth himself shall be exalted."

I can fancy some self-righteous one, trusting in his own goodness, priding himself on his outward observances, but with his heart firmly closed against the humbling truths of the gospel—I can fancy such an one living on contented and self-satisfied. Sickness comes upon him; but it makes no impression. Death draws near; but he remains unchanged. I can fancy him taking his place before "the great white throne," still confident, still full of his own deservings. But presently a voice is heard, saying, "How camest thou in hither, not having on the wedding garment?" Ah, then he will be speechless, and his proud heart will sink within him. He has "exalted himself," and he will now be "abased."

I can fancy another, of a meek and lowly character, confessing himself to be "less than the least of all saints," not worthy to be called a servant of Christ—feeling that he deserves nothing at God's hands—bowed down under a sense of sin, and hardly daring to hope that

Christ would accept such an one as he is—growing in grace and holiness, but still wishing to be counted nothing but a humble penitent—I can fancy the joy of such an one, when the Saviour shall honour him before the assembled world, and "give him a place and a name better than of sons and daughters." Then it will be found that God "raiseth up the poor out of the dust, and lifteth up the beggar from the dunghill, to set them among princes, and to make them inherit the throne of glory." Then too will the truth of these words be seen, "He that humbleth himself shall be exalted."

Look once more at the Parable. "When thou art bidden," says our Lord, "go and sit down in the lowest room."

We are bidden to a feast—to the gospel feast. We are invited to be the friends and guests of Christ. Let us go and take "the lowest room." Let all our pride be put away. Let us seek to be clothed with humility. A low place is the fittest for a sinner; and the more grace we have in our hearts, the lower we shall stoop, and the more humble will be our walk with God. What did Jesus say to His disciples? "Except ye be converted, and become as little children, ye shall not enter into the kingdom of heaven."

Go, thou contrite sinner—go, thou pardoned believer—go, thou follower of the meek and lowly Saviour—go and take thy proper place—" the lowest room."

And let me now give you just a few directions on this subject. I speak to those of you who have found Christ and salvation through Him.

1st. Never forget that you owe all you have, and all you are, to God's grace alone. St. Paul never lost sight of this. He was ever ready to say, "By the grace of God I am what I am."

When we feel that we are sinful and vile, and that we deserve nothing but eternal death, *then* how wonderful and glorious does the love of God appear in providing salvation for us! Can *you* feel this? Does your heart go along with me, whilst you are reading these pages? And can you say, "Blessed be God He *has* taught me this. I see it clearly. I am nothing; and infinite mercy alone has rescued me from what I so richly deserved"?

2dly. It is not enough to consider *ourselves* nothing; but we should also be willing to be *thought nothing of by others.* If true grace is at work within, we shall have such a view of the secrets of our own evil hearts, and of the purity and holiness of God, that we shall not *wish* to be thought better than we really are. In fact the flattery of our fellow-men will be painful and sickening to us.

And yet how hard it is to keep clear of this snare! How hard to crucify our old nature in this respect! I dare say there are some here who often pray that God may humble them, and lower them, in their own eyes—and to do even this requires grace. But how few of us go a step further, and ask God to lower us in the eyes of *others!* To do this does indeed need *much* grace.

The day is soon coming, when we shall be taken off the false heights we have been standing on, and be set on our true level—when the esteem of others shall vanish and pass away like smoke, and we shall be just what God finds us to be—neither more nor less.

3dly. We should try and *think well of others*. St. Paul gives his Christian brethren this advice, "Let each esteem other better than himself"—"in honour preferring one another."

Whenever you see a person who takes every opportunity to cry down his brethren, mark that for a proud and unhumbled person. You may be sure that he does it, in order to exalt himself. But when you see any one anxious to hide his brother's failings—unwilling to expose all his little defects—you will generally find that to be a humble person, who deeply feels the many faults in his own character.

And if it is delightful to *see* this kind, large-hearted, Christian spirit in our brethren, let us earnestly seek to *have it ourselves*. Let us ask God to root out every jealous feeling from our hearts, and enable us to take real pleasure in discovering whatever is good in others.

4thly. Never *thrust yourself into notice.* A pushing, forward person cannot have much of the spirit of Christ.

Do what is right, because it is right, and because it is pleasing to God; but do not court the approval of others. This was the sin into which the Pharisees fell; for they "loved the praise of men more than the praise of God."

The meek and lowly follower of Christ will wish to avoid observation as much as possible. If, for instance, he gives money away in charity, he will do it as quietly as he can, according to the Saviour's rule, "Let not thy left hand know what thy right hand doeth." If he prays, he will not wish all the world to know it. If he comes to the house of God, he will go quietly to his place, and there he will pour out his heart before the Lord; for he comes here not to be seen of men, but to offer up his unworthy prayers to the Father of mercies, and to listen to His gospel message of love. Or, if he talks on religious subjects, he will say as little as may be about himself, and much about the love of his Redeemer. If however he *does* speak about himself, it will not be to show what a good Christian he is, but rather to show how unworthy he is, and to display the riches of God's grace in saving one so undeserving.

Oh that we may become more truly humble! Whatever company we are in, whether among men of the world, or among the people of God, let us be content to take "the lowest room." And if God shall be pleased hereafter in His great mercy to exalt us, and to say to us, "Friend, come up higher," there will be no pride *then* to mingle with our joy; but as many of us as have been redeemed by the blood of Christ will then fall down before Him to whom we owe so much—casting our crowns before His throne—never uttering one boastful word of our own worthiness; but for ever saying, "Worthy is the Lamb that was slain to receive honour, and glory, and blessing"!

THE LOST SHEEP.

Luke xv. 3—7.

" And he spake this parable unto them, saying, What man of you, having an hundred sheep, if he lose one of them, doth not leave the ninety and nine in the wilderness, and go after that which is lost, until he find it? And when he hath found it, he layeth it on his shoulders, rejoicing. And when he cometh home, he calleth together his friends and neighbours, saying unto them, Rejoice with me; for I have found my sheep which was lost. I say unto you, that likewise joy shall be in heaven over one sinner that repenteth, more than over ninety and nine just persons, which need no repentance."

(See also Matt. xviii. 12—14.)

HERE is the owner of a flock brought before us. He possesses an hundred sheep; and he is represented as going after *one that has strayed*. So anxious is he to recover the wanderer, that he leaves the rest in the wilderness—that is, in the pasture where they are feeding—and turns all his thoughts towards the lost one. He spares no pains, and counts no toil too great, to recover it. And when at length, to his great joy, he discovers it, he seizes it, lest it should wander further, lays it on his shoulders, and carries it home in safety. His joy is so great, that he invites his friends and neighbours to share it with him.

Such is this beautiful and simple Parable— so beautiful, that every time we read it, it gives us fresh pleasure; and so simple, that the most unlearned has no difficulty in understanding it. But lest we should miss its meaning, Jesus is pleased to give us the key to it in the seventh verse—" I say unto you, that likewise joy shall be in heaven over one sinner that repenteth, more than over ninety and nine just persons, which need no repentance."

Such, our Lord Himself tells us, is the truth which the Parable is intended to teach us. By the straying sheep is meant *the lost sinner*. By the return to the fold is meant *the sinner's repentance*. By the ninety and nine in the wilderness is meant *those who need no repent-*

ance. And by the rejoicing of the friends and neighbours is meant *the joy in heaven when a soul is saved.*

But our Lord gives us no help at all in finding out who *the Shepherd* is, who cares so lovingly, and has done so much, for his sheep. No; He leaves us to *guess* that, for He knows that we cannot well guess wrongly.

Now we will take the several points as they come.

1st. *The stray sheep.* It leaves the safe fold. It turns away from the pasture, where the flock is feeding. It wanders over hill and dale, seeking nourishment. It is exposed to danger; but still it wanders on, getting farther and farther from its home.

Is it not just so with the Sinner—not merely with some *great* sinner, but with *us all?* "All we, like sheep, have gone astray," says the Prophet. And our Church echoes the same words, "We have erred and strayed from thy ways like lost sheep."

How wonderful it is that, although God is so gracious to us—although He has provided such rich and abundant blessings for us in

His fold—although we know that the nearer we are to Him, the greater is our peace—yet we *will* depart from Him; we choose the evil and refuse the good. Yes, and when we have smarted for our folly, and see the danger of being at a distance from God, still we wander on farther and farther from our true home. And just as one stray sheep leads others astray, so it is with us. First Eve strayed; then Adam; and all we have followed in the same trodden path of evil.

It is possible that *you* may be astray *now*. Your conscience may tell you that you are afar off from God at this moment. Ah, if the sheep's danger is great, wandering alone and helpless on the mountains, exposed to every foe, and far removed from the shepherd's care, what must be *your* danger—without God in the world—without Christ—having put away your only Protector? The Lost Sheep in the Parable just describes your condition; and most forlorn and miserable it is!

But, blessed be God, you *need* not stray one moment longer. There is a way back to the fold. There is a voice that calls you. For, observe

2dly. *The return of the sheep.* This describes the *sinner's repentance.*

Some alas! wander on till they are lost for ever; for the longer we are away from the fold, the less desire we have to return. We get to love the very taste of sin, and to hate the paths of godliness. Oh, how hard we grow —how wedded to our evil ways—how callous to our danger!

It is indeed a great mercy, if grace stops us in our sinful course, and softens us in repentance. What a miracle of mercy it is, if any of us have found our way back! What a blessing, if we can say, " We *were* as sheep going astray; but are *now* returned to the shepherd and bishop of our souls"!

That was a miracle which restored the poor sickly Leper to health—which made the Palsied man take up his bed and walk—which called Lazarus from his grave. But it is as great, or even a greater wonder, when a leprous *soul* is cleansed, a corrupt *heart* changed, a dead *sinner* raised to the newness of life. O Lord, do Thou work many such miracles in this our day!

3dly. There was great rejoicing when *the sheep was brought back*—joy on the Shepherd's part, and joy among his friends. This describes the feeling of Christ and of His Church, when any sinner is converted, and any soul is saved.

There is joy *in heaven*. The news is brought there, and a thrill of gladness runs through that blest abode. Angels and Archangels rejoice; for "are they not all ministering spirits, sent forth to minister for them who shall be heirs of salvation?" Saved souls rejoice; for they well know the blessedness of salvation. Christ rejoices; for He then "sees the travail of his soul": it was for this He shed His blood, and drank the bitter cup of suffering.

Aye, and there is joy too *on earth*. For who can be so selfish as not to experience a feeling of thankfulness, when a sinner is brought into the fold of Christ—when a poor lost sheep joins the " little flock " ?

But the Shepherd in the Parable seemed to feel more joy over this recovered sheep, than over the rest of his flock, which were already safe. Can we not understand this? Suppose one of your children is very ill; and you have passed many an anxious hour in watching over it; sometimes despairing of its recovery, sometimes hoping almost against hope. Its spirit seems to flutter between life and death.

But suddenly, as you sit by its bedside, its little eyelids close, and it falls into a sweet sleep. There is a change for the better; and now health begins to return. Oh, would you not rejoice over that recovered child *more* than over all the rest? You love the others. You always have loved them. You are thankful for their health. But still, *more* thankful are you for that little sufferer; for it has been given back to you, when it seemed to be on the point of leaving you. Such is in some measure the joy that is felt when a sinner repents.

But who are "*the ninety and nine*" sheep in the wilderness? Our Lord says they are those who "need *no repentance.*" Some consider this to mean the Pharisees and those who *fancy* they need no repentance. Others take it as describing the Angels, who have never strayed. But I am disposed to think that our Lord means by it those who *have* repented—whom He numbers among His people —and who, though now on earth, are safe in His hands. It is true, we all need daily repentance. But the repentance spoken of here seems to be that great inward change, when the sinner is brought to know Christ, and heartily to love Him—that repentance which we commonly call Conversion.

4thly. There is one more point, to which I must call your attention. See how this happy state of things is *brought about*. The lost sheep does not return of its own accord. It does not find its own way back. There is one, who cares for it, who goes after it, follows it up, and, when at length he finds it, deals tenderly with it, and brings it home rejoicing. There is *but One* whom this picture describes—He who deserves indeed to be called "the Good Shepherd"—who giveth His life for the sheep, and loves them as no other loves them. Why was it that Jesus left the glory of heaven, and came into this wilderness-world? Was it not to seek and to save the lost? Was it not as a shepherd going after his wandering sheep?

And how does He search us, and call us

back? It is by His *Word:* that is the Shepherd's *voice.* It is by *affliction:* that is the Shepherd's *crook,* by which He lays hold of us, and pulls us back—roughly, it may be, but still lovingly. Yes, He often uses chastisement as a means of bringing us into the fold of safety. He does not willingly afflict us, but He is sometimes forced to adopt this method.

One may fancy a Shepherd, on some dark and stormy night, very anxious to bring his scattered sheep into the fold. He throws the door wide open, but they will not enter. He calls them, but to no purpose. He drives them, but when they get close to the open door, they turn aside. Having tried many means, we may fancy him at length resorting to this—he takes one of their number, bears it on his shoulder, and enters with it himself into the fold; and then the bleating flock, one after another, follow him.

So, the Good Shepherd is sometimes forced to act with us. He snatches away some one very dear to us—a child, a parent, a brother—and takes him to heaven before us, that we, who have so often refused His call, may now at length follow Him, and enter in.

O sinner, Jesus is searching for thee, as it were—searching for thee now. He longs to save thee. He desires to have thee with Him where He is. Oh yield yourself to Him at once. Pray to Him in the words of the Psalmist, "I have gone astray like a lost sheep. Seek thy servant."

I cannot do better than conclude my remarks on this Parable with the following beautiful lines:—

>I was wandering and weary,
>When the Saviour came unto me;
>For the paths of sin grew dreary,
>And the world had ceased to woo me.
> And I thought I heard Him say,
> As He came along His way,
> Ye wand'ring souls come near me;
> My sheep should never fear me;
>   I am the Shepherd true.
>
>At first I would not hearken,
>And put off till to-morrow;
>But life began to darken,
>And I was sick with sorrow.
> And I thought I heard Him say, &c.

At last I paused to listen;
That voice could not deceive me;
I saw His kind eyes glisten,
So anxious to relieve me.
   And I'm sure I heard Him say, &c.

He bore me on His shoulder,
And tenderly He brought me;
Then bade my love grow bolder,
And said how He had sought me.
   And I thought I heard Him say, &c.

I feared His love might weaken,
And fail, when more He knew me;
But it burneth like a beacon,
And its light and heat go through me.
   And I'm sure I heard Him say, &c.

Let us do then, dearest Brother,
What will best and longest please us —
Follow not the ways of others,
But give ourselves to Jesus.
   If we follow on His way,
   We may always hear Him say,
   Come, little flock, come near me;
   My sheep should never fear me;
      I am the Shepherd true.

THE PRODIGAL SON.
PART I.

LUKE xv. 11—19.

"And he said, A certain man had two sons: and the younger of them said to his father, Father, give me the portion of goods that falleth to me. And he divided unto them his living. And not many days after the younger son gathered all together, and took his journey into a far country, and there wasted his substance with riotous living. And when he had spent all, there arose a mighty famine in that land; and he began to be in want. And he went and joined himself to a citizen of that country; and he sent him into his fields to feed swine. And he would fain have filled his belly with the husks that the swine did eat: and no man gave unto him. And when he came to himself, he said, How many hired servants of my father's have bread enough and to spare, and I perish with hunger! I will arise and go to my father, and will say unto him, Father, I have sinned against heaven, and before thee, and am no more worthy to be called thy son: make me as one of thy hired servants."

THE PRODIGAL SON. 215

Our Lord's Parables are, each and all of them, most beautiful. They are like so many gems dotted about the page of Scripture. But this Parable is of all perhaps the brightest and most full of light. It shines out among the rest with special brilliancy. "We might call it (says a Christian writer) the pearl and crown of all the parables." There is no other which speaks so touchingly of the misery of sin, and of the exceeding love of God to those who mourn over it.

The story is this—

There are two sons living in their Father's house. The Younger of them is dissatisfied with his home, and is bent on leaving it. He therefore obtains from his Father the portion of goods which falls to his share, and departs. He wanders into a far country in search of happiness. But he does not find it. On the contrary he soon gets into trouble. His money is spent, and he finds himself destitute, and in the midst of strangers who care not for him. He is forced to work for his daily bread. And so low is he brought, that he actually feels the pangs of hunger, and is almost ready to devour the food intended for the swine.

In this extremity, the thought of his past folly, and of the home which he has left, comes into his mind. "How many hired servants of my Father's (thought he) have bread enough and to spare, and I perish with hunger!" He wakes up, like one from a sleep, and determines no longer to lead this miserable life. He resolves to go back, and throw himself at his Father's feet, and implore his forgiveness.

Here the first portion of the Parable ends. We have seen what the "earthly story" is: now for the "heavenly meaning."

In that poor, foolish Son, we have a picture of the Sinner—a picture of ourselves. We have left our Father's house. We have wandered and strayed from His ways, like lost sheep—not some of us, but all. "*All* we, like sheep, have gone astray; we have turned *every one* to his own way." "We are very far gone (says one of the Articles of our Church) from original righteousness"—*i.e.*, the righteousness in which God first created us.

Do we not know well enough that there is a Home, a holy, happy Home, where our Father dwells? And yet, from this Home, we have gone further and further away, ever since the days of our childhood. We have loved the World, the "far country," better than we have loved Heaven. We have tried its pleasures. We have expected much from them; but have found them emptiness. We have been feeding upon "husks."

Well is it, if we have smarted for our folly. Well is it, if we have felt our misery. Well is it, if that feeling of want, which the Parable speaks of, has been our experience. Better to be in want, to grieve, to be thoroughly wretched—better to taste the bitter pangs of spiritual hunger — than to say, "All is well: I am rich, and increased with goods, and have need of nothing."

We are told that the thoughtless, careless, pleasure-seeking Prodigal "came to himself." He was not himself before. He had acted as a madman. He had given himself up to folly. He had plunged blindly into sin; and he had bitterly smarted for it. But now he comes to his senses. And was not his want, his wretchedness, a blessing to him? If he had never felt that, he would probably have remained an outcast still.

A person may be in a state of sin, and his soul may be in danger: and yet he may be satisfied to go on as he is. He may have no longing for the Home that he has left, and no desire to return. He may live on at enmity with God; and yet have no misgivings, no remorse as he looks back, and no dread when he thinks of the future. His eyes may be altogether blinded, and his conscience seared, as with a hot iron. His life may be a kind of dream. And yet all the while "the wrath of God abideth on him."

Then, I say, it is far better to feel our misery, than to fancy we are happy—better that the cup should taste very bitter, than that we should go on drinking it. Thank God for any means, however painful, which bring us to our senses. He is our best friend, who shows us our wounds and sores, and sends us to the great Healer.

If you had seen the Prodigal in the fields

tending the swine, with his tattered garments, and his haggard, downcast look, you would no doubt have pitied him. How different from what he once was! How altered! What a wreck of his former self! But was it not better for him to have suffered—better to have been so reduced—than to have gone on in his bad course, with the world smiling upon him? Adversity was better for him than prosperity.

And here we cannot but call to mind the case of Manasseh, King of Judah, so like this case of the Prodigal. He, as you know, fell into sin. He departed from God. And for many years he followed the leadings of his own wicked heart. At length affliction came —a sore affliction. And this brought him to his senses. "And when he was in affliction (we are told) he besought the Lord his God, and humbled himself greatly before the God of his fathers, and prayed unto him. And he was entreated of him, and heard his supplication. *Then* Manasseh knew that the Lord he was God."

Affliction was the saving of Manasseh. And so it is sometimes with ourselves. Oh, *that* is a blessed trial (whatever it may be) which brings us to our bearings—which leads us to God. Some will, I think, agree with me in this. Some can say, "It is good for me to have been afflicted. Before I was afflicted, I went wrong, but now have I kept thy word. Blessed was that Sermon, or that verse of Scripture—yea, and blessed even (we may say) was that Accident which stopped me short — or that Fever which confined me so long to my sick-room—or that Disappointment, which blasted my earthly hopes, and brought me to myself. It was the Lord's doing, and I thank Him for it."

But sometimes Affliction comes, and yet the heart remains untouched.

Now Manasseh's was a *felt* affliction, and so was the Prodigal's. His heart ached, his spirit was fairly broken. And so must it also be with us. We must feel that we are ready to perish—that we have not a husk to eat—not a rag to cover us—that we are utterly destitute. Then shall we be willing to throw ourselves, in all our misery and emptiness, on Him who is "the Sinner's Friend."

You will observe that nothing is said in the Parable about *the way* by which the Prodigal was brought to a better mind. Affliction was the principal means: but affliction alone did not produce the change. All that we are told is, that "he came to himself." Are we to gather from this, that the sinner *of his own accord* sees his folly, and repents? Certainly not. As well might we expect a blind man to restore himself to sight, or a dead man to give himself life. The Parable does not tell us so—but I should think it likely that the Father did not leave his prodigal child to himself. He probably sent after him many a message—wrote many a touching word to him—and used other means to rouse him from his folly. And so too God follows the Sinner, in his course of sin, speaks to him by His Word, by His Ministers, in a thousand ways. He draws us "with the cords of a man, with the bands of love." His language is, "How shall I give thee up, Ephraim? How shall I deliver thee, Israel?

Mine heart is turned within me." God does not leave the sinner, until the cup of his iniquity is full. He does not withdraw the checks and workings of His grace, till the heart is hopelessly hardened, and the conscience deadened.

But there was something more than a sense of wretchedness in the case of this Prodigal. There were some better feelings as well. His thoughts now turned to his Father's house. He longed to be once more there. Not that he dared hope for those same rich blessings which he once enjoyed. A place among his Father's servants was all he seemed to look for—" How many hired servants of my Father's have bread enough and to spare, and I perish with hunger!" "Oh that I could have a place among them! Oh that I could fare as they are faring! Make me as one of them!"

It is a happy thing for the sinner, when he begins to feel even the slightest longing for a better portion—when he is heartily weary of living a godless life, and pines after a purer happiness than this world can give him. If we have that desire, it is God who has kindled it in our hearts. Pray that it may never leave us till we have found our happiness in Christ.

There is "bread enough" for all in our Father's house—food for the hungry soul, strength for the weak and weary, comfort for the sorrowful, pardon for the guilty, a welcome for the penitent.

There are many gathered there—many happy ones already sheltered in those blessed mansions. And yet there is room—room for every single soul that seeks admission.

Yes, my dear Brother or Sister, there is room for *you*—" bread enough, and to spare." Do not live on, as you perhaps have been living, away from God, and from Christ, and from peace. "Return unto the Lord thy God; for thou hast fallen by thine iniquity. Take with you words, and turn to the Lord. Say unto him, Receive us graciously." "Make me as one of thy hired servants."

I have said that the Prodigal felt uneasiness at his present condition, and longed for something better. But he did not stop there. He formed *a resolution* in his own mind—a determination to go at once, and cast himself at his Father's feet—" I will arise, and go to my Father."

This was a noble resolve. For just think how deep he was sunk in profligacy, and how hard it was to get loose from all his sinful entanglements. He had joined himself moreover "to a citizen of that country;" and there was some difficulty in breaking away from his service.

But, in spite of all this, he felt, "I must go. *Here* I am starving: *there*, in my Father's house, there is plenty. *Here* I am miserable: *there* my broken heart may yet be healed. *Here* I am perishing: *there* there is deliverance and safety."

It does indeed require a strong resolution to leave the path of sin. We get wedded to our evil habits. We get so to love our bad ways, that we cannot easily part with them. The world binds us with its twisted cords. Satan holds us in his net, and it is very difficult for us to escape.

For example, we will suppose that a person has been accustomed to indulge in some amusement, which is altogether unsuited to a Christian. It requires no little courage to say, "That is not the recreation for me. I will turn from it; and never from this day will I indulge in it again." Or, if any one has been in the habit of staying away from God's house, it is no easy matter to turn over a new leaf, and become a regular church-goer. Or, if he has loose and ungodly companions, it is a great trial to say to them, "I see things differently to what I once did. I cannot fall in with your ways now. I must leave you, and seek the companionship of those who fear God."

But this must be done. We must make a strong resolution in our own minds, that, cost what it may, we will forsake sin, and seek our happiness in the Lord. The struggle may be hard. But how great will be our joy, when we can say, "Our soul is escaped as a bird out of the snare of the fowler: the snare is broken, and we are delivered."

Perhaps you have already made such resolutions. Perhaps you can remember many a determination to which you have come at different times in your life. But they were broken again, and all fell to the ground. Such has been the case with hundreds—ah, with hundreds now in hell!

Are such resolutions then wrong? Are they useless? No, they are neither wrong, nor useless. But let us in future do this—let us remember how utterly weak we are, and let us make all our resolutions, *God helping us*. Let us throw ourselves on the Lord, and beg of Him to give us grace and strength to carry them out. And most assuredly He will give us the desired help. His strength will be made perfect in our weakness.

And here we must leave the Prodigal for the present—having come to himself—having reflected on his deplorable condition—and having resolved at once to go, and implore forgiveness from him whom he had so long forsaken.

Now, some one who is reading this may perhaps be ready to exclaim, "That thoughtless Prodigal is just the very likeness of myself. My Saviour has painted that picture, as it were, for me. In that mirror I see no other than myself. I have been seeking my happiness away from God—far off from my proper Home. And I have indeed suffered for my folly. I am without God, and without grace.

I am destitute. The husks of this world afford no nourishment to my soul. I long for better food."

Believe me, a time of hunger will come to every soul, whether we now feel it or not. And oh the misery of feeling it, when it is too late to satisfy it. There is spiritual food in abundance, suited to our wants. And God loves to " satisfy the empty soul, and fill the hungry soul with goodness."

Or, it may be, you are one who has " tasted the good word of God, and the powers of the world to come"; but you have fallen back, and are now minding earthly things. I do not ask if you are happy: I know you cannot be. No swine's food, nor anything of this world, can satisfy a soul that has been awakened. Go at once, and cast yourself at your Father's feet. Seek again the happiness you once enjoyed in His blessed service. Christ is the only real food. He is the Bread of life—the Bread of Eternity. Take Him for your true support, and you will hunger no more. " Your soul shall be satisfied as with marrow and fatness; and your mouth shall praise him with joyful lips."

THE PRODIGAL SON.
PART II.

LUKE XV. 20—32.

"And he arose, and came to his father. But when he was yet a great way off, his father saw him, and had compassion, and ran, and fell on his neck, and kissed him. And the son said unto him, Father, I have sinned against heaven, and in thy sight, and am no more worthy to be called thy son. But the father said to his servants, Bring forth the best robe, and put it on him; and put a ring on his hand, and shoes on his feet: and bring hither the fatted calf, and kill it; and let us eat, and be merry: for this my son was dead, and is alive again; he was lost, and is found. And they began to be merry. Now his elder son was in the field: and as he came and drew nigh to the house, he heard musick and dancing. And he called one of the servants, and asked what these things meant. And he said unto him, Thy brother is come; and thy father hath killed the fatted calf, because he hath received him safe and sound. And he was angry, and would not go in: therefore came his father out, and intreated him. And he answering said to his father, Lo, these many years do I serve thee, neither transgressed I at any time thy commandment: and yet thou never gavest me a kid, that I might make merry with my friends: but as soon as this thy son was come, which hath devoured thy living with harlots, thou hast killed for him the fatted calf. And he said unto him, Son, thou art ever with me, and all that I have is thine. It was meet that we should make merry, and be glad: for this thy brother was dead, and is alive again; and was lost, and is found.

LET us now examine the remainder of this Parable. We left the Prodigal with the firm resolution in his mind to go and throw himself at his Father's feet, and implore his forgiveness.

He had come to himself. He had seen his folly. He had felt his wretchedness. He had resolved to return home, if indeed one so utterly undeserving could find acceptance. He is already on his way. His face is turned towards his Father's house; and his mind is probably filled with many an anxious thought —" How will my Father receive me? What will be his feelings towards his rebel Son? I remember how kind he was to me in days gone by—how tender—how loving. I remember the treatment I *used* to receive from him. But since then he may be changed towards me. I have so long abused his goodness, and so often thwarted his wishes. Ah, if I have my deserts, I shall be rejected. His door will be shut, and his heart closed, against me."

On he goes however towards the well-known spot of his earlier days. Every field, every house, every tree reminds him of the happiness he once enjoyed. But can that happiness be ever again his portion? He probably sends forward a message to say that he is on his way. And before he gets within sight of home, he sees in the distance his Father coming forth to meet him. This encourages him; and as he draws near, he judges from his Father's countenance that he has the same heart towards him that he ever had—that the same feeling of love still dwells within him—and that years of waywardness and ingratitude have not quenched it. And as his Father runs towards him, and falls on his neck, and embraces him, he seems to say, "Father, I deserve not all this. I have sinned against heaven and in thy sight, and am no more worthy to be called thy son."

He felt at that moment as if nothing would be too bad for him. All that he had hoped for was the lowest place in his Father's household. He knew that even this would be more than he deserved. What must have been his surprise then, when his Father " said to his servants, Bring forth the best robe and put it on him; and put a ring on his hand, and shoes on his feet: and bring hither the fatted calf, and kill it; and let us eat, and be merry: for this my son was dead, and is alive again; he was lost, and is found."

Let us now leave the Prodigal for a moment, and think of the Sinner, as our Lord would have us do.

Here we have indeed a most blessed picture of *a Returning Penitent*, and of his acceptance. When grace has humbled us, and shown us our sinfulness and our misery, then we feel a desire to return to our Father. We go to Him with fear and trembling, for we feel that we deserve nothing but wrath. We hardly dare to approach Him; and yet we are told that He is full of mercy. We say to Him, what we have often said before with our lips—but now we say it from our hearts—" Father, I have sinned against heaven, and before thee, and am no more worthy to be called thy son."

Has this deep, earnest cry ever come from you? Has your heart ever bled from a consciousuess of sin? Have you ever knelt down alone, and poured your trouble into God's ear? Have you ever told Him that your sins grieve you, and that you desire above all things to obtain His forgiveness? Feeling that Jesus has shed His blood for you, have you taken your burden to the throne of grace, and found relief there?

Oh the kindness of our heavenly Father! When we are yet a great way off, He comes forth to meet us. He is ready to forgive us. Words of pardon are on His lips. He brings forth the best robe to cover our nakedness. And are we not told in this very chapter, that " there is joy in heaven over one sinner that repenteth"? Our heavenly Father Himself rejoices; for another child is welcomed into His family. Our Saviour rejoices; for "he sees of the travail of his soul, and is satisfied." The Angels rejoice; for "are they not all ministering spirits, sent forth to minister for them who shall be heirs of salvation"?

And shall not *we* rejoice too, when a soul is brought home to God—when one dead in sins is raised to newness of life—when a lost one is found?

We do not think enough about *others*. We do not pray for them enough. We are most of us too much shut up within ourselves. Oh for more thought about our brethren who are yet astray! Oh for more thought about the Church of Christ, and those who are being gathered into it! Oh for more concern about those prodigals, who are still in the far country!

Ah, the night is dark, and they are a long way from home. Shall we not stretch out a hand to them, to lead them into the right path? Shall we not whisper to them, "This is the way; walk ye in it"—"Here is the path of safety; turn not from it: it leads to your Father's House"?

We may do something, each of us. And what an unspeakable blessing to be the means of leading one—only one—into the right road! Think what it is to share the very joy of heaven, by bringing one sinner to repentance!

But there is another Person in the Parable, to whom our attention is now drawn, who could feel none of this joy. I mean *the Elder Son*.

When his Younger Brother took his journey into the far country, *he* appears to have remained at home. And now, amidst all the rejoicing at his Brother's unexpected return, he alone rejoices not. He was in the field at the time, engaged in his daily work. And hearing the sounds of unusual gladness, he asks the cause. And when they tell him what it is, instead of lifting up his heart with thankfulness, a feeling of anger comes over him, and he refuses to take part in the general joy of the household. His Brother is come —his long-lost Brother—but he cares not for him. He has been kindly received: this only stirs up his jealousy. His Father comes out, and entreats him to join the rest; but to no purpose. "Lo, these many years do I serve thee," was his pettish reply, "neither transgressed I at any time thy commandment: and yet thou never gavest *me* a kid, that I might make merry with my friends. But as soon as this thy son was come, which hath devoured thy living with harlots, thou hast killed for him the fatted calf."

His Father reasons with him, "Son, thou art ever with me, and all that I have is thine. It was meet that we should make merry and be glad; for this thy brother was dead, and is alive again; and was lost, and is found."

Now, to whom does the close of this Parable refer? Whom does this *Elder Brother* represent?

Some have thought that God's true and faithful people are here described; for you observe that the Father says, "Son, thou art *ever with me,* and all that I have is thine." This certainly at first sight looks a little like the language of approval. But then, is there not something very sour and churlish in the conduct of the Elder Son—something which is hardly in keeping with the character of a true child of God? Could any one, whose heart was right, have felt as he did towards his sorrow-stricken, but now accepted, Brother? And can any true Christian grudge the favour shown towards a returning penitent, and be displeased at God's exercise of mercy?

Certainly not. Surely then we have here, not the spirit of a Christian, but rather the spirit of a boasting, self-righteous, disdainful Pharisee. He exclaims in the pride of his heart, " Lo, these many years do I serve thee; neither transgressed I at any time thy commandment." And then, pointing with contempt to his poor fallen Brother, he rakes up all his past guilt, and scorns the idea of giving him such a welcome—" This thy son, which hath devoured thy living with harlots—thou hast killed for him the fatted calf"!

Does not this remind us of the Pharisee in the Temple, boasting of his good deeds, and thanking God that he was not as other men, or even as that poor penitent Publican by his side? The two pictures seem to describe the very same person.

And then, in our Parable, the Father takes his Elder Son on his own showing—" True, my son, your conduct has been outwardly correct. As far as *outward* service goes, you always have been near me and with me; and all the privileges of my family have been yours. Surely you have nothing to complain of, but ought rather heartily to take part in our joy."

It is clear then to my own mind that our Lord must have referred to the Pharisees in this part of the Parable. And oh let us beware of the hard, contemptuous spirit shown by this Elder Brother. Watch against it. Learn to rejoice in another's welfare. Take an interest in the salvation of your fellow-men. Be not extreme to mark what they have done amiss; but rather be disposed to throw a cloak over their failings, and be thankful if they show the least desire to return to their Father's house.

I have now set the whole Parable before you. It is full of instruction, and full of encouragement. It gives us a most blessed view of God as our Father, and shows how ready He is to gather us under the shelter of His love.

We are all like the Prodigal, inasmuch as we have all wandered and strayed from the ways of God. Are we like him in his recovery —in his return? Have we experienced the joy of forgiveness? Have we "tasted that the Lord is gracious"?

Oh how wondrous is that love! How overflowing is that mercy! *We* may look upon the sinner's case as hopeless. *He himself* may fear that he has gone too far to be restored—that God's feelings towards him are feelings of anger—that He is ready to meet him with the sword of vengeance. But no; "God is love." "He retaineth not his anger for ever; but he delighteth in mercy." He still yearns over His wandering child with a Father's pity. "Is Ephraim my dear son? Since I spake against him, I do remember him still. Therefore my bowels are troubled for him. I will surely have mercy upon him, saith the Lord."

And have we not reason—all of us, even though we may have found forgiveness— have we not reason to use again and again the language of this penitent son? We are for ever grieving our heavenly Father; and I believe the holier we are, the more we shall feel the greatness of our sin against

Him, and our daily, hourly need of forgiveness. Our Church has done well then to place the Prodigal's confession at the very beginning of our Public Service; as if to teach us that we have need to confess our sins, and to seek for pardon, every time that we approach God.

The joy of the accepted Prodigal was great, and such too is the joy of the forgiven sinner. But there is a joy even greater than his joy— namely that which the established Believer feels. His peace flows on like a calm, placid river. His mind is stayed upon God. He feels now that his Father loves him, and his delight is to do His will. But he looks for still greater happiness—still purer joy—in his Father's Home above.

THE SHEPHERD AND THE SHEEPFOLD.

JOHN x. 1—9.

"Verily, verily, I say unto you, He that entereth not by the door into the sheepfold, but climbeth up some other way, the same is a thief and a robber. But he that entereth in by the door is the shepherd of the sheep. To him the porter openeth; and the sheep hear his voice: and he calleth his own sheep by name, and leadeth them out. And when he putteth forth his own sheep, he goeth before them, and the sheep follow him: for they know his voice. And a stranger will they not follow, but will flee from him: for they know not the voice of strangers. This parable spake Jesus unto them: but they understood not what things they were which he spake unto them. Then said Jesus unto them again, Verily, verily, I say unto you, I am the door of the sheep. All that ever came before me are thieves and robbers: but the sheep did not hear them. I am the door: by me if any man enter in, he shall be saved, and shall go in and out, and find pasture."

It is a little doubtful whether this should be reckoned as one of our Lord's Parables or not. Certainly *the whole chapter* cannot be considered as a Parable; but I think the first nine verses may. At all events, what is said in the sixth verse will justify us in treating it as one—" This *Parable* spake Jesus unto them."

Our Lord pictures before us a Sheepfold —not such a fold as we are accustomed to see in this country, made of a few hurdles fastened together; but an enclosure built up with high walls, so as to prevent the possibility of any attack from wild beasts or other enemies.

Now, into such a Fold as this, if we were to see any one entering, not by the door, but either by breaking down the wall, or climbing over, we should at once suspect that he could have no good intentions. Such a person is here described. " He that entereth *not by the door* into the sheepfold, but climbeth up some other way, the same is a thief and a robber." The Shepherd will naturally enter *by the door;* and to him the person stationed at the door, the Porter, will at once open; and the sheep will welcome their Shepherd, and feel that he is no stranger.

It is clear that our Lord was levelling this Parable against the Jewish Teachers, and perhaps especially against the Pharisees. They professed to be the Guides and Leaders of the people; but they were untrue and unfaithful Shepherds—starving, instead of feeding, the flock—administering poison to them, rather than wholesome nourishment.

At the end of the Ninth Chapter, we find that some of the Pharisees, who were with our Lord, and heard His words, were greatly offended at what He had said, exclaiming, " Are we blind also?"—we who have prided ourselves on seeing more clearly than others— are we blind also? Upon which Jesus replied, saying, " If *ye were* blind, ye should have no sin; but now *ye say,* We see; therefore your sin remaineth." And then He proceeds to speak this Parable, in which He compares them to false shepherds, who had forced their way into the sheepfold, and had not entered by the appointed door.

But let us look again at the Parable. Our Lord goes on to say in verse 8, "All that ever came before me are thieves and robbers: but the sheep did not hear them." Now, what did He mean by this? Surely not that *all* those Teachers who had gone before were false Teachers. He did not mean to condemn such as Moses, and Elijah, and Isaiah, and John the Baptist. No; such could not be His meaning. What He meant was, that all who had taught what was *contrary to His truth*—all who had led men by ways which were *not His ways*, however fair their speech, and however promising their professions, were but as thieves and robbers: they came only "to steal, and to kill, and to destroy;" not to save.

But, as for our Lord Himself, how different was *His* character! "I am the *good* Shepherd," He says. And then, to the close of the chapter, or at least to the end of verse 27, He enters upon this beautiful comparison of a Shepherd, and tells us what He has done for

His beloved flock, and what are the peculiar marks of His true sheep.

But in reading this Parable, we have often perhaps found a difficulty in getting a clear view of its meaning. And I think it is for this reason—because our Lord here uses *two* comparisons. He speaks of Himself both as the *Shepherd*, and also as the *Door* of the sheepfold. But if we read the passage attentively, we shall see *why* He does so. Look at verse 6 : "This parable spake Jesus unto them : but they understood not what things they were which he spake unto them. Then said Jesus unto them again, Verily, verily, I say unto you, I am *the door* of the sheep." They could not take in what He had said about them as "thieves and robbers," and about Himself as the good and true Shepherd; for men are generally slow to understand what makes against themselves. And in consequence of this dulness on their parts He changes this comparison, and speaks of Himself under another likeness, "I am the *Door*."

Having now explained the chief difficulties

which are in the Parable, it will be well to touch on some of the leading points contained in it—such as the Fold, the Flock, the False Shepherds, the true One, the Door. I will say a word or two upon each.

First, I will speak about *the Fold*. What is the Fold into which Christ gathers His sheep—the fold of safety—the fold from which He leads us forth to find pasture for our souls? That Fold is *the Christian Church*.

Christ does not leave His people to wander alone up and down this world. He bands them together in one great company, which He calls His Church. He provides pasturage for them—spiritual nurture—and defends and guards them under His watchful care. "When he ascended up on high, he gave gifts unto men. And he gave some apostles, and some prophets, and some evangelists, and some pastors and teachers; for the perfecting of the saints, for the work of the ministry, for the edifying of the body of Christ."

But the Church on earth is not our dwelling-place for ever. It is only our *preparation-home*. There is a better Fold above, into which He will one day welcome all His chosen ones, where they will be as one united flock, in the very presence of their Shepherd.

Be thankful for the Church in which you are now sheltered. I do not mean the building. I mean the Company of God's people, to which you are joined. I mean that Church, which provides you with Ministers, which teaches you sound doctrine, which puts right words into your mouth, which guides you on the pathway to heaven. The folded Sheep become attached to the very enclosure which gives them shelter. And we should love our Church, as we would love the Mother who cares for us, bears us in her arms, and hides us in her bosom. We should be thankful for the means of grace so mercifully provided for us. We should use them as helps by the way, till we are permitted to join " the general assembly and church of the first-born, which are written in heaven."

Secondly, I will say a word or two about *the Sheep*, which compose this Fold. They are those who have entered into Christ's Church at Baptism. We were then numbered among the Saviour's flock. He gathered us into His arms, and received us into His bosom.

Oh that we all valued this high privilege! Oh that we all loved our Shepherd, and were *true* members of His flock! But alas we have wandered and strayed from the right path, and have turned each one to his own way. And some never return. The Fold has no charm for them. They have no taste for the pleasant pastures, into which the Saviour would lead them; and they never reach the Fold above.

Are *we* among the Saviour's sheep? Have we His mark upon us—the mark of God's elect? Is our spot "the spot of His children"? If so, although the world may not know us; *He* knows us, and we know Him. And we can look up, and say, "The Lord is my shepherd: I shall not want. He maketh me to lie down in green pastures; he leadeth me beside the still waters."

Thirdly, there are *False Shepherds*, of whom the Parable speaks. There were many of these in our Lord's day, and there are many now. Satan has his agents in the world, as well as Christ — powerful, willing, active agents. There are those who are bent on doing his work. It may be, they are in the sheepfold, among the sheep, but they have not entered by the door. They are opposed to Christ, and hate His gospel. Instead of leading men *to* Him, they draw them *from* Him.

There are many such Teachers in the present day. You meet them in the railway. You hear them in the streets of London. You read their words in the infidel newspaper.

How sad to be destroyers, instead of healers—to scatter poisoned seed, instead of truth—to ruin men's souls, instead of saving them!

May *we* know and love the voice of the good Shepherd! May it have brought such peace to our souls, that the voice of false shepherds may grate upon our ears, and we may flee from it as from the voice of strangers! Let the words of our Collect be often upon our lips, " O Almighty God, grant that thy Church, being always preserved from false

Apostles, may be ordered and guided by faithful and true pastors."

But, fourthly, Who is *the True Shepherd?* I need say but little on this. For if you examine what our Lord says of Himself, in the remaining verses of this chapter, it will plainly shew you how great and glorious a Shepherd He is. Think of Him caring for His sheep—laying down His life for them—going before them, as I have sometimes seen a shepherd putting himself at the head of his flock, and leading them on into this or that pasture-field—not driving them, but leading them—not forcing them to follow him, but gently calling them with his voice of love.

Such is *our* Shepherd. Safe indeed, and happy, is our condition, if we are living near to Him, trusting His gracious care, and looking to Him for daily and hourly keeping.

There is one more point to touch upon—*the Door*. Jesus, as we have seen, is both the Shepherd of the sheep, and also the Door of the Fold.

He is the Door. Then you and I cannot

draw near to God—we cannot make one step towards the Fold—except through Him. "No man cometh unto the Father *but by me.*"

"I am the Door." Blessed be His name for having told us this! If Christ had not given Himself for us, then Heaven would have been like a high sheepfold, which no man could enter. We might seek to climb up, but in vain. We should be treated only as thieves and robbers. But now each one of us may enter by the open door. We have only to ask, to seek, to knock, and it shall be opened unto us.

And how blessed will it be, when we reach the Fold above! There will be no dangers to terrify us there—no lack of pasture there—no false shepherds there—no solitary ones there. The Sheep and the Shepherd will be together: "he that sitteth on the throne shall *dwell among them.*" We may be parted from one another here. Our happy ties may be broken asunder. But if they are Christian ties, they will be again renewed. We shall be as one family in our Father's house—one Fold and one Shepherd.

THE DISHONEST STEWARD.

LUKE XVI. 1—12.

"And he said also unto his disciples, There was a certain rich man, which had a steward; and the same was accused unto him that he had wasted his goods. And he called him, and said unto him, How is it that I hear this of thee? give an account of thy stewardship; for thou mayest be no longer steward. Then the steward said within himself, What shall I do? for my lord taketh away from me the stewardship: I cannot dig; to beg I am ashamed. I am resolved what to do, that, when I am put out of the stewardship, they may receive me into their houses. So he called every one of his lord's debtors unto him, and said unto the first, How much owest thou unto my lord? And he said, An hundred measures of oil. And he said unto him, Take thy bill, and sit down quickly, and write fifty. Then said he to another, And how much owest thou? And he said, An hundred measures of wheat. And he said unto him, Take thy bill, and write fourscore. And

252 THE DISHONEST STEWARD.

the lord commended the unjust steward, because he had done wisely : for the children of this world are in their generation wiser than the children of light. And I say unto you, Make to yourselves friends of the mammon of unrighteousness ; that, when ye fail, they may receive you into everlasting habitations. He that is faithful in that which is least is faithful also in much : and he that is unjust in the least is unjust also in much. If therefore ye have not been faithful in the unrighteous mammon, who will commit to your trust the true riches ? And if ye have not been faithful in that which is another man's, who shall give you that which is your own ?"

This is perhaps the most difficult of all the Parables. And yet, when we come to look closely into it, I believe that most of the difficulties will disappear. It is one of those passages of Scripture, which quite repay us for giving our whole attention to them.

Only St. Luke relates the Parable. And we can find no particular circumstance which led to its being spoken, as we have found in many others; for it follows close upon the Parable of the Prodigal Son.

Let us then turn to the words themselves, and see if we can discover any one verse, which will serve as a key to the whole. In verse 8 we have, I think, exactly what we want. This verse at once tells us what was our Lord's object. It was to show that the children of God may learn a lesson of spiritual wisdom even from the bad conduct of worldly men— or, to put it in another way, that men are far keener and more alive to their worldly interests, than they are to those important matters which concern their souls. "The children of this world are in their generation wiser than the children of light." Let us keep this key-verse in mind, and it will greatly help us to understand the Parable.

And now for the Parable itself. The chief Person who is brought before us is a Steward, who managed the estate of a certain rich man. An accusation is brought against him of having betrayed his trust, and wasted his lord's property, employing it for his own selfish ends, and not for his master's benefit.

The man's guilt being clearly proved, he is desired to make up his accounts, and resign his stewardship. This is a heavy blow to him; and he begins immediately to turn over in his mind how he can provide for his future maintenance, when he shall be dismissed from his office. He has never been used to day labour; and to beg his bread would be a disgrace. His mind is soon made up. He hits upon a plan, which, though a most dishonest one, certainly shews that he is fully alive to his own interests. He determines to make friends with all those who owed anything to his master, so that he may reckon on their receiving him under their roof when he is dismissed.

Upon this, he calls together all who owed any rent or money to his lord, and makes his proposal to each in turn. He asks the first how his account stands—" How much owest thou unto my lord?" He replies, "An hundred measures of oil." Then says the Steward, "Call it fifty—Take thy bill, and sit down quickly, and write fifty." You will observe it was the custom to pay in kind, and not in money, as we do. He then calls another, "And how much owest thou?" He answers, "An hundred measures of wheat." He proposes to him to strike off twenty measures, reducing the debt to eighty—"Take thy bill, and write fourscore." And so with the rest. You see, he lowered the sums due to his employer, in order to secure for himself the good services of those who were to be gainers by this dishonest transaction.

Now, an act of dishonesty is generally found out. It was so in this case. It soon came to the master's ears. And though of course he was greatly shocked by his steward's conduct, and though he was much grieved at his dishonesty, he could not help giving him credit for his *worldly wisdom and shrewdness*. "The lord *commended* the unjust steward"—not because he had done *rightly*—but "because he had done *wisely*." And then Jesus adds His own remark upon it—"The children of this world are in their generation wiser than the children of light."

So far, I trust, all is now pretty clear to you as regards the actual Parable. But there are a few things connected with it, which require some consideration.

The first stone that people generally stumble at is the expression, "The lord commended the unjust steward." They imagine that it is *our Lord* Himself who commends him. This however is not the case. It is *the Steward's lord*, or master. Put away then at once this mistake from your minds. And again remember *what* his master commends him for—not for his conduct generally, for from this he had greatly suffered, but only for *his cleverness.*

The next difficult point is at the close of the Parable, where Jesus gives us this advice —" And I say unto you, Make to yourselves friends of the mammon of unrighteousness; that, when ye fail, they may receive you into everlasting habitations."

What did our blessed Lord mean by this? By "the unrighteous mammon," or, as it is here called, "the mammon of unrighteousness," He meant worldly riches. Now, these are worthless in themselves, and are positively a snare to many. They have ruined thousands. But He would have us turn them to good account, making a blessing of them, instead of a curse. If, for instance, we possess worldly goods, we should so employ them as to further the glory of God, and the welfare of men, so that when we die, we may be received into heaven.

Joseph of Arimathæa was a rich man. And among other things, he built for himself a new sepulchre. There was perhaps some little pride in this. But when he becomes a Christian man, he turns his riches to a good account. He " makes friends of the mammon of unrighteousness" by laying it out for the Saviour whom he loved.

Mary too " made friends of the mammon of unrighteousness " when she bought some ointment, which in itself was worthless, and anointed the feet of her Lord, thus testifying her love for Him.

The poor Widow also, who spent her last farthing by casting it into the Lord's treasury, thus " made friends," as it were, " of the mammon of unrighteousness."

This, I think, is the meaning of the ninth verse.

But there is a yet further difficulty in the three next verses—" He that is faithful in that which is least is faithful also in much: and he that is unjust in the least is unjust also in much. If therefore ye have not been faithful in the unrighteous mammon, who will commit to your trust the true riches? And if ye have not been faithful in that which is another man's, who shall give you that which is your own?" I can fancy some of you being a little perplexed by these words. Let us examine them.

"He that is faithful in that which is least is faithful also in much"—that is, The man who is honest and trustworthy in little matters will be so in great ones; and he that is unjust in little matters will be unjust also in greater ones. The Steward wronged his lord as to a few measures of corn and oil: and most likely he would not have scrupled to wrong him to a much larger extent, if only he had had the opportunity. And so again, if we act unfaithfully as to worldly things, how can we hope that God will entrust to us the far greater things of His kingdom. If we do not use aright our present gifts and blessings, we cannot expect that He will commit to us the true riches of His grace. And further, our Lord says, "If ye have not been faithful in that which is another man's, who shall give you that which is your own?" As much as to say, Worldly advantages are intrusted to men as stewards. They are not our own, but we are to employ them for God. If then we are not faithful in the use of these, is it likely that He will give us the treasures of heaven, which, if once ours, we shall possess for ever?

Thus I have endeavoured to give you the best explanation in my power of this difficult Parable, and of our Lord's words at the end of it. If, bearing in mind what has been said, you will read it again with care, I trust you will be able to understand its meaning.

But now let us turn this important Parable inward upon ourselves, so that we may not lose the great lessons which it was intended to teach us. First it seems to teach us that we are *all Stewards*, and God is our Master. We are not our own, but His. We are not sent here to live as we please, but to do the will of Him that sent us. Our blessings, and our advantages, and our opportunities are entrusted to us to be employed in God's service.

Our *money* for instance, whether we have much or little of it, is not our own—it is merely lent to us. This is not a way of talking: it is the truth. If I have a few pence in my possession, or as many pounds, I am answerable to God for the way in which I expend them. For this, among other things, I must render an account.

Our *time* too is not our own. God gives it to us, but only for a while—just so long as He pleases. He may call it back at any moment. Never think that you may do what you please with your hours and your days. Are you spending them merely on your own pleasure, or in your own way? Are you forgetting that you are but a Steward, and that you have a Master who employs you? Perhaps the day is not far off, when you will long to call back even one wasted hour, that you may spend it on the great concerns of your soul.

Our *influence* again, whether it be great or small, we must use for God. Are there not some, who are doing no good in the world— some who are doing positive harm. Oh bear in mind that the Master's eye is upon you— that you are a Steward—and that "it is required of stewards that a man be found faithful." I am a steward, and so are you.

May each of us fulfil our office, so that, when our Lord appears, " we may not be ashamed before him at his coming "!

Secondly, the day is near when it will be said to you and me, " *Give an account* of thy stewardship; for thou mayest be no longer steward." When a few more summers shall have shone upon us—when a few more birthdays shall have come round—but oh we must not speak of so long a time as this—when a few more *weeks* perhaps, or even *days*, shall have passed away, our stewardship will be at an end for ever. There will be no more opportunities *then;* but we must go before God just as we are. Think of this, and remember that our account will be a very strict one, for to whom much is given, of him will much be required. " Strive to enter in at the strait gate; for many will seek to enter in, and shall not be able."

But there is one more lesson which the Parable teaches. We may call it *the great lesson* of the Parable. I mean, that we should be just as anxious about our everlasting welfare, as many are about their worldly interests. How eager men are about their gains, and their pleasures, and their earthly advantages! They will even sacrifice their health to obtain them. And yet, when they have got all that they have so eagerly sought for, it perishes in the using. Truly there are many worldly and ungodly men, who fairly put to shame the people of God, by running with more eagerness to death and ruin, than *they* do to life and happiness. But let us learn a lesson from them. Let them not have all the earnestness on their side. Let us be as eager for eternal life. Let us be as earnest for salvation. Let us be as wise in "laying up a treasure in the heavens that faileth not." Let us so live in this world, that when death comes, and this poor dwelling of ours crumbles to dust, we may be received into those everlasting mansions, where Christ is gone to prepare a place for us.

THE RICH MAN AND LAZARUS.

Luke xvi. 19—31.

"There was a certain rich man, which was clothed in purple and fine linen, and fared sumptuously every day: and there was a certain beggar named Lazarus, which was laid at his gate, full of sores, and desiring to be fed with the crumbs which fell from the rich man's table: moreover the dogs came and licked his sores. And it came to pass, that the beggar died, and was carried by the angels into Abraham's bosom: the rich man also died, and was buried; and in hell he lift up his eyes, being in torments, and seeth Abraham afar off, and Lazarus in his bosom. And he cried and said, Father Abraham, have mercy on me, and send Lazarus, that he may dip the tip of his finger in water, and cool my tongue; for I am tormented in this flame. But Abraham said, Son, remember that thou in thy lifetime receivedst thy good things, and likewise Lazarus evil things: but now he is comforted, and thou art tormented. And beside all this, between us and you there is a great gulf fixed: so that they which would pass from hence to you cannot; neither can they pass to us, that would come from thence. Then he said, I pray thee therefore, father, that thou wouldest send him to my father's house: for I have five brethren; that he may testify unto them, lest they also come into this place of torment. Abraham saith unto him, They have Moses and the prophets; let them hear them. And he said, Nay, father Abraham; but if one went unto them from the dead, they will repent. And he said unto him, If they hear not Moses and the prophets, neither will they be persuaded, though one rose from the dead."

THIS is the only Parable which gives us an insight into the state of men in the unseen world.

Let us consider,

1st. The condition in which the Rich Man and Lazarus were placed *in this life;* and

2dly. The portion allotted to each of them *in the next.*

First, then, we have here the earthly history

of two men, very different, both as regards their worldly station, and also their spiritual condition.

The one was "a Rich man, which was clothed in purple and fine linen, and fared sumptuously every day." We may picture him to ourselves as inhabiting a lordly mansion, in the enjoyment of all the good things that money could procure for him, living for this world, and for this world only.

The other was a poor Beggar, who was laid at the rich man's gate, glad enough to receive now and then some of the broken bits, which were left from his table. And he was not only poor, but afflicted with sickness and disease. He had no doctor to dress his wounds, and no kind friends to comfort him. But "the dogs came and licked his sores."

Now, if we could have seen these two men, would not some of us have been disposed, at first sight, to envy the rich man's condition, and to pity the miserable state of the other? But if so, we should be forgetting the fact, that perhaps under "the purple and fine linen" of the one, there existed a cold and unloving heart, full of cares and disappointments, and utterly devoid of that true peace, which belongs to God's people. We should be forgetting that under the tattered garment of the other, there was perhaps a happy and contented spirit: and though he had no one to cure his outward diseases, he had found a true Physician, who could heal his inward sores, and pour balm into his spiritual wounds.

The Rich Man's motto was, "Let us eat and drink, for to-morrow we die." His table was crowded with the choicest food; his appetite pampered with every delicacy. But meanwhile his soul was neglected, and his God despised. He was clothed in purple—the royal colour; but he never sought for that robe which would cover the nakedness of his soul. He never hungered for that food which endureth unto everlasting life. No; for his treasure was on earth, and his heart there also. "The god of this world" had "blinded his eyes," so that he could see nothing beyond the present.

But when we turn to Lazarus, what a different picture do we behold—miserable in his outward appearance, and wanting the necessaries of life. Without friends or comforters, he found pity only from the dumb animals about him: "the dogs came, and licked his sores." Whilst the Rich Man was clothed "with purple and fine linen," *he* was covered only with ulcers. Whilst the Rich Man "fared sumptuously every day," *he* desired to be fed with "crumbs": the one probably waited upon by a number of servants; the other with the dogs for his attendants.

But amidst these woes, this want, this wretchedness, poor Lazarus was not forsaken. That eye, which never slumbers nor sleeps, was fixed upon him. That arm, so mighty to save, was stretched out over him. And, as we shall presently see, for this friendless outcast a place was prepared among Saints and Angels in the mansions of heaven. He sat as a Beggar at the Rich Man's gate. But he also "sat at the feet of Jesus"—a beggar even there, but not a rejected one; for he could ask, and have; he could knock, and the door of shelter was opened to him. Here he found a Friend, with whom the

Rich Man was unacquainted—just such a Friend too as he wanted—one that never turned a deaf ear to his complaint—who could soothe his troubles, and supply his wants—who never sent him empty away.

Do *you* possess such a Friend as Lazarus had? Are *you* acquainted with Him who has said, "I am with you always;" "I will not leave you comfortless"—who can feed you, when your soul is hungry, and can give you joy, when sorrow presses hard upon you—who, when you are bruised from head to foot with "wounds and putrefying sores," can heal you with His love—and when He sees you disfigured by the filthiness of sin, says to you, "I will sprinkle clean water upon you, and ye shall be clean; from all your filthiness and all your idols will I cleanse you"? Can you look up, and say, "O God, thou art *my* God:" "Jesus, thou art *my* Saviour:" "Thou, Lord, art *my* shepherd; I shall not want"?

But the Parable does not stop with the *earthly* life of these two men. It carries us a step or two beyond. They both die. The

Beggar is taken first; and is "carried by angels into Abraham's bosom." What a mighty change for him! But a moment before no man served, or waited upon, him; only the dogs apparently cared for him. But now Angels are in attendance, and carry him to the bliss prepared for him. Not one Angel, but many, are there, each rejoicing to bear such a burden. And whither do they carry him? Into Abraham's bosom—that place of untold happiness, where Abraham is!

The Rich Man also dies; and it is added, he "was buried." He had perhaps a costly funeral, befitting his rank. There was probably a long train of followers; but there were no rejoicing angels ready to carry him to Paradise. His lifeless clay was laid in a splendid sepulchre. But where was his soul? Did it remain in its earthly tabernacle? Did it rest in peace? Did he, who had once gained almost the whole world, now find that his wealth could do anything for him? Could it procure his pardon? Could money purchase for him the key which unlocks the gate of heaven? No: hear the sad description given of his fate—" The Rich Man also died, and was buried. And in hell he lifted up his eyes, being in torments." Surely death was no pleasant messenger to him. " The clods of the valley" were not " sweet" to him. For in that valley he had no shepherd to guide his sinking steps; no rod, and no staff, to comfort him. Having closed his eyes to all that was dear to him here below, he opened them in a place of torment! And as if to add to his remorse and misery, he sees Abraham afar off, and Lazarus—happy Larazus—" in his bosom "—safe in that blessed place, where, as our Prayer-book says, " the souls of the faithful, after they are delivered from the burden of the flesh, are in joy and felicity."

In the Parable a conversation is given between the lost man and Abraham. Not as though such a conversation could actually have taken place; but in order to shew us something of the wretchedness of a soul ruined for ever.

Notice the expression of this man's anguish —his hopeless misery. He does not ask to be released from his fiery prison; for he knows the bars of it are closed on him *for ever*. But he asks in agony for a drop of water to cool his tongue. He asks that Lazarus may bring it—Lazarus, whom he once despised, but whom he now envies. His request however, small as it is, is rejected. It cannot be. Not even one moment's relief can be given from his pain. No messenger can be dispatched to cool, even for an instant, that burning tongue. "Between us and you," said Abraham, "there is a great gulf fixed; so that they which would pass from hence to you cannot, neither can they pass to us that would come from thence."

What a fearful truth is here declared to us! There will be a hopeless and eternal separation between the lost in hell and the saved in heaven. There will be no change then. The day of grace will then be closed; the time of mercy over. *Now* we may, by God's grace, pass from a sinful course to a holy walk with God. We may *now* escape from shipwreck, and gain the shore of safety. We may *now* flee from the wrath to come, and find shelter in Christ. But *then* it will be too late. There will be "a great gulf fixed." He that is "unjust" will be "unjust still"; and he that is "filthy" will be "filthy still"; the sinner's state will be fixed, and that for ever.

But the Rich Man was not only filled with remorse at his own past life: he was also tormented with the agonizing thought of his Brethren, who were likely soon to follow him. This added a most bitter sting to his misery. He cannot get out of his mind their perilous condition. He remembers perhaps that he had often encouraged them in their thoughtlessness; and the recollection of this haunts him. Though *his own* sad lot is fixed, can nothing be done to rescue *them?* Can no messenger be sent, to warn *them*, lest they also come into that place of torment?

No, it cannot be. Abraham answers him, "They have Moses and the Prophets; let them hear them." That is, they have the Bible: what need they more? If they continue to reject that, they are without excuse.

Once more he urges his request—" Nay, father Abraham; but if one went unto them from the dead, they will repent." Again he refuses, saying, "It they hear not Moses and the Prophets, neither will they be persuaded, though one rose from the dead."

We think sometimes that a Messenger, if sent from the other world, would come with a power which nothing could resist—that the stoutest sinner would tremble—that the slumberer would start up, and cry for mercy —that the unbeliever would be convinced. But no; for we have already abundance of light, if we will but walk in it. If men reject the message, which God has already sent them, " neither will they be persuaded though one rose from the dead."

And now let us look back on the Parable, and see what more we may gather from it.

1st. We may gather that *the Rich are not always happy*, though they may *seem* to be so. That Rich Man, whom we have been thinking of, living in his lordly house, with his princely dress and his sumptuous fare, was not I dare say half so happy *even here*, as his poor ragged neighbour. For he knew not God. He enjoyed not the presence of his Saviour. And then, when his last sickness came, how miserable was his prospect! Little enough was the happiness he was going to leave behind him; but great was the misery before him—an awful blank—a dismal future—a world unknown—of which the forebodings already filled him with terror. No; we have no cause to envy the wealthy, unless they are also " rich towards God."

2dly. *The poorest may find comfort.* " Hearken, my beloved brethren, hath not God chosen the poor of this world rich in faith, and heirs of the kingdom which God hath promised to them that love him "?

Lazarus in his rags—Lazarus with his sores —Lazarus with the sweepings only of the Rich Man's table—often hungry and cold, and without any one to cast an eye of pity on him—poor Lazarus must at times have felt that his was a hard lot. But then there was one Friend, who never left him—who in his dreariest moments had words of comfort to whisper in his ear, and was making ready a glorious home for him above.

If you know what want is, may you also know Him who can cheer you in your sadness, can relieve you in the hour of your deepest distress, and will not lay upon you more than you can bear. Oh say unto Him,

"I will trust, and not be afraid; for thou, Lord, art my strength and my song."

3dly. Neither Poverty or Riches *have anything to do with our state hereafter*. The Rich Man in the Parable was not condemned for being rich; but for having *wasted* his riches—for having made them his god, and spent them unprofitably—for having laid up his treasure upon earth.

Neither again, was Lazarus accepted merely because he was poor, and suffered much. It was not his poverty which recommended him to God. It was not the misery or lowness of his condition. But it was that "godliness, which is great riches"—that lowliness of heart, which led him in all humility to seek a Saviour for his soul. This was the reason, the true reason, why Abraham said to the miserable sufferer before him, "Now he is comforted, and thou art tormented."

4thly. At death *we instantly become either happy or miserable*. The Rich man's change was immediate. There was no pause—no sleeping in the grave for a while. His worthless *body* slept there; but *he himself* "lifted up his eyes, being in torments." And with Lazarus too the change was *immediate*. He was instantly conveyed by angels to Abraham's bosom. And so it was too with the Penitent Thief on the cross, "*To-day* thou shalt be with me in Paradise." And St. Paul, when thinking of his own departure, speaks of being *at once* with his Saviour— "desiring to depart, and to be *with Christ*," "willing rather to be absent from the body, and *present with the Lord*."

It is clear then, that when we die, we shall instantly wake up in a state of happiness or misery—to be with Christ for ever, or with the devil and his angels.

Lastly, let us take a hint from this Parable, that if we would warn our brethren it must be *now*. It may be, we ourselves are encouraging them in sin. Or, if we do not actually *encourage* them, we have never, it may be, taken a single step to *check* them. Ah, if we are lost hereafter, it will add a pang to our misery, when we remember that instead of stopping them, we rather helped them forward, in their evil course. Oh the anguish of feeling, as we lie upon a death-bed, that we have not only ruined ourselves, but have ruined others also —that we have not only rushed to destruction ourselves, but have dragged others with us!

On the other hand, if we have found mercy for our own souls, let us do all we can to bring others to the fountain of mercy too. If we know of a Brother, or a Child, or a Friend, or a Companion, or even a Stranger, who is travelling on that broad and beaten track which leads to hell, shall we not send after him one cry of warning? Shall we not make one kind, loving effort to stop him in his heedless course? Shall we not put up an earnest prayer to God, that He will be pleased to touch his heart, and snatch him "as a brand from the burning?"

THE WIDOW AND THE JUDGE.

LUKE XVIII. 1—8.

"And he spake a parable unto them to this end, that men ought always to pray, and not to faint; saying, There was in a city a judge, which feared not God, neither regarded man : and there was a widow in that city; and she came unto him, saying, Avenge me of mine adversary. And he would not for a while : but afterward he said within himself, Though I fear not God, nor regard man; yet because this widow troubleth me, I will avenge her, lest by her continual coming she weary me. And the Lord said, Hear what the unjust judge saith. And shall not God avenge his own elect, which cry day and night unto him, though he bear long with them? I tell you that he will avenge them speedily. Nevertheless when the Son of man cometh, shall he find faith on the earth?"

THE object or end of this Parable is told in the first verse. It was "spoken," St. Luke says, "to this end, that men ought always to pray, and not to faint."

This at once shows us what was passing in our Lord's mind. Knowing how backward we are in coming to God, and how easily we persuade ourselves to give up prayer, and to imagine that it is useless, He shows us by a Parable that if we press our claims, we are sure to obtain our requests from God. He shows us what earnest, believing, persevering prayer will do for us, by bringing before us the case of a poor Widow, who, by dint of her continued and pressing intreaties, induced even a wicked Judge to listen to her complaint.

There lived, He says, in a certain town a Judge. This man was of a hard and selfish character. He had no fear of God, and no feeling for his fellow-men. And there was also in that same city a poor helpless and friendless Widow, who had been trampled upon and wronged by one of her neighbours. Perhaps he owed her money, and refused to pay her; or he may have unjustly injured her character, which was dearer to her than money.

He had in some way or other taken advantage of her weak and helpless condition, and had acted unjustly towards her.

There was not much hope of getting this Judge to undertake her cause, but still she goes to him. At first he turns a deaf ear to her complaint. She gets no redress. How was it likely she should from one who neither "feared God nor regarded man"? Her errand seemed to be a hopeless one; and many would have given all up in despair. But she perseveres. And the more closely he stops his ears, the more loudly she entreats him.

At length he gives way—not because he felt the justice of her request—not because his heart was touched by her exceeding earnestness—but because she fairly wore him out by her continued applications to him. "He would not for a while: but afterward he said within himself, Though I fear not God nor regard man, yet because this widow troubleth me, I will avenge her, lest by her continual coming she weary me."

Now, it is very easy to understand this

Parable; for, like most of our Lord's teaching, it is beautifully simple. And yet there is a right and a wrong way of explaining it.

If I was to say, This Widow represents the sinner, and this Judge represents God—that would, I think, be a wrong explanation; for what two beings can be more unlike than this churlish, unjust Judge, and a gracious, holy God, whose ear is ever open to His people, and who is so ready to help them in their need?

Sometimes a thing is made clear to us by a similitude, or likeness; as for instance when Christ is compared to a Shepherd, or the Gospel to a Feast. But sometimes also a thing may be explained by a contrast, or unlikeness —something that is just the very contrary to it—as in the case before us. If this unjust man is persuaded to do justice to this poor Widow against his own wicked and selfish feelings, how much more will God listen to our complaints, since He is the very opposite —a God of love and goodness! "And the Lord said, Hear what the unjust judge saith. And shall not God avenge his own elect which cry day and night unto him, though he bear long with them? I tell you that he will avenge them speedily."

The teaching of the Parable is this—If earnest, persevering entreaty, such as this Widow used, could move a selfish and hardhearted Judge, how much more will a just and holy God, a Father of mercies, listen to the continued prayer of those whom He loves.

And now let us get what good we can both from the Parable, and from our Lord's words at the close of it. May He Himself bestow His blessed Spirit to guide and teach us!

"Men ought to pray," says Jesus, in the first verse. They ought to pray for two reasons, because,

First, their need is very great and very pressing. How great are our bodily wants! We have got *health* perhaps; do we not want it to be continued to us? And yet no care or precaution will ensure it. We must ask God then day by day to preserve us in health. We want *food* too. But some will say, I have food in my house for my present wants, and I have money to buy more. Still we have need to pray day after day,

"Give us this day our daily bread." God can deprive us in an instant of all we have. If our barns are ever so full, or our cupboards ever so well stored, God can at any time bring hunger and want upon us, if He pleases. We want *success* in our business, whatever it be. Well, we are perhaps industrious and far-sighted. But this will do but little, unless God blesses our endeavours; "Except the Lord build the house, they labour in vain that build it: except the Lord keep the city, the watchman waketh but in vain."

Ah, and how great are the wants of our souls! People do not feel those wants till God opens their eyes and their hearts. But oh how great they are! Do we not want pardon for our sins—our many sins—those sins which make God so angry with us—those sins which close up heaven against us? Do we not want a Saviour, whose blood can cleanse us, whose righteousness can cover us, whose grace can strengthen us, whose love can bind up all our wounds, and gladden our hearts? Do we not want a Teacher to instruct us, a Guide to lead us, a Comforter to cheer us, a Sanctifier to make us pure within? Do we not want the Holy Spirit to dwell within us? Then indeed " we ought to pray."

Again, we should pray, because God *expects* it of us. He bids us pray. Though He knows what is suitable for us better even than we know ourselves—though He is acquainted with all our wants even before we tell them out to Him—yet He will be asked before He gives. "I will be *enquired of*," He says, "for these things." "*Call* unto me, and I will answer thee." "*Ask*, and it shall be given you." "Whatsoever ye shall *ask* in prayer, believing, ye shall receive."

Men ought then to pray, first because their wants are great, and next because God bids them pray, and "the prayer of the upright is his delight."

But Jesus says, "Men ought *always* to pray." There is no time when prayer is out of season. There is no spot on this side the grave where prayer is out of place. Thank God, we may pray when alone, or when with others, when in our chamber, or when in the fields. In times of joy we may pray, or when the dark cloud of sorrow hangs over us. When God seems near to us, we may pray, and ask Him to abide with us; or when He seems to be afar off, we may entreat Him to come near to us and bless us. Yes, whatever be our wants, or difficulties, or trials, or dangers, God's ear is always open to attend to the words of our complaints. Thank God, He has said that we may "*always* pray."

And we find the Apostles urging this in their Epistles—this habit of *always* praying. In writing to the Thessalonians, St. Paul says, "Pray *without ceasing:* in *everything* give thanks." And to the Ephesians he says, "Praying *always* with all prayer and supplication in the Spirit."

This may seem a hard command to some. Yes, it is a hard thing for a worldly, unconverted man to pray at all. It is a burden to him to do it even now and then. But to be *always* praying—this is intolerable. When God however gives us His Holy Spirit to dwell within us, then Prayer becomes our delight; we feel it to be a great mercy that we may draw near to a gracious Father, and tell Him of all our wants.

This prayerful spirit is the mark of God's children. They cry day and night unto Him. An old writer makes this beautiful remark, "The whole life of the faithful," he says, "should be one great connected prayer"; and again, "Prayer should be the salt which is to season everything."

May God give us a more praying spirit! May He teach us that the more we are in His presence the happier we are! May we feel as David felt, "My soul thirsteth for God, the living God!"

But our Lord, in the passage before us, adds that men "ought not to *faint*"; that is, They ought not to be discouraged, though God may seem not to hearken to their supplications. I say *seem*, because God always *does* hear the prayers of His people. Yes, and He always *answers* our prayers, if we pray according to His will, though His answer may not come immediately.

We ought not then to faint or be discouraged, but to believe and persevere. The poor Widow had but one weapon, and that was persevering prayer; but by it she prevailed. By her continued entreaties she at length won over the man, who at first seemed so unlikely to be moved by them.

We have a beautiful instance of this in the case of the Syrophenician Woman, mentioned in the Gospels. She comes to our Lord, and for a while He appears not to heed her, like the Judge in the Parable. But she prays on boldly and hopefully. She is nothing daunted by His seeming indifference. And at length her anxiety is relieved: He sends her away with her request granted. He yielded, not as the Judge did, because He was wearied by her earnestness, but because He loved to meet her with a blessing, and because He only waited in order to try her faith.

We very often find a difficulty with these poor unbelieving hearts of ours, to pray at all. But still more difficult do we find it to *go on* praying, when the desired answer does not come. For instance, we ask for a blessing on our own souls. We pray for more faith, more love, more power to resist temptation, for brighter views of Christ, for a more rejoicing hope. But our hands still hang down, and our knees are still feeble. God seems no nearer to us. Ah, this sorely tries our confidence. But let us pray on. The gift *will* come. "Though it tarry, wait for it: it will surely come."

Or, again, we draw near to the throne of grace for a dear Friend, or a Relative, or a Neighbour. We entreat God to change his heart, and wash his soul. But we see him still going on frowardly in his ways; his heart remains untouched. What are we to do? Shall we give over? Shall we leave him to himself? No; we "ought to pray, and not to faint." This Parable is our encouragement.

See how plainly we are told that God is willing to hear the prayers of His people. Will He pay no heed to them? says our Lord. Will He not "avenge his own elect, who cry day and night unto him"? They may be persecuted and oppressed in a thousand ways; but He loves them. They are unspeakably dear to Him. They are often disposed to cry in their distress, "O God, how long shall the adversary do this dishonour? Why withdrawest thou thy hand? Why pluckest thou not thy right hand out of thy bosom to destroy the enemy?" But never—no never—do they speak to Him in vain. He may seem not to notice their wants. But He will avenge them, and that certainly, seasonably, *speedily*—not one moment later than is good for them. Perhaps He may see it well to keep them waiting, as He did His disciples in the storm; but He will come at last, though it be not till "the fourth watch in the night;" and *then* He will deliver them.

Our Lord finishes with these remarkable words, "Nevertheless"—notwithstanding God's promise to His people—"when the Son of man cometh, will he find faith on the earth?" He knew there was at that time not much faith in the world. And, looking forward to His coming again, it grieved Him to think how little of this faith there would be even then—this faith which shews itself in persevering prayer—this faith which hopes even against hope.

May this faith be found in you and me! May we, like the Widow, or like the Syrophenician Woman, call upon the Saviour with untiring earnestness! May we, like Jacob, wrestle with our God in prayer, and "not let him go except he bless us"!

THE PHARISEE AND PUBLICAN.

LUKE XVIII. 9—14.

"He spake this parable unto certain which trusted in themselves that they were righteous, and despised others: Two men went up into the temple to pray; the one a Pharisee, and the other a publican. The Pharisee stood and prayed thus with himself, God, I thank thee, that I am not as other men are, extortioners, unjust, adulterers, or even as this publican. I fast twice in the week, I give tithes of all that I possess. And the publican, standing afar off, would not lift up so much as his eyes unto heaven, but smote upon his breast, saying, God be merciful to me a sinner. I tell you, this man went down to his house justified rather than the other."

THE very first of these verses tells us what this Parable is about. We are told that Jesus "spake this parable unto certain which *trusted in themselves that they were righteous, and despised others.*"

Here then we have the class of persons

whom our Lord intended to condemn—*the Self-righteous*.

For this purpose He places before us two men, who both go up to the House of God, but in a very different state of mind. The one was a proud Pharisee: the other a despised Publican.

Now, the sect of the Pharisees was the strictest, and most religious, sect among the Jews. They were very exact about outward observances—more so than about the inward condition of the heart; and they looked down with great contempt upon all who did not belong to their own party.

The Publicans, as you probably know, were a kind of Tax-gatherers — a set of people very much hated and scorned by the Jews—and many of them persons of indifferent character. So much so, that the name became almost a bye-word. Thus our Lord says, when speaking of one who walks disorderly, "Let him be unto thee as a heathen man, or *a Publican*"—as much as to say, Let him be an outcast from your company.

But, however low these men were, God's grace could reach them. Here and there a penitent Publican joined himself to the flock of Christ, and became a true disciple. In the next chapter, for instance, we read of Zacchæus, who was one of them, becoming a follower of Jesus. Matthew too was a Publican; and when Christ called him, he was "sitting at the receipt of customs"— at the office where the taxes or customs were paid.

One can hardly fancy two more opposite characters than these men who went up to the temple to pray—"the one a Pharisee, and the other a publican."

We will first take the Pharisee. He goes into the House of God, full of self-confidence — his heart swelling with pride. There he stands, in some spot where he may be seen—without a single misgiving—without a thought that there can be anything wanting in him. He presently looks around, and casts a scornful eye on his fellow-worshipper, the poor brow-beaten Publican.

And now mark his Prayer. "God, I thank thee"—he begins. So far all is well enough. It is well to give a large portion of our devotions to the expression of our thankfulness. But what does he thank God for? Not for his many mercies and blessings; but he says, "I thank thee that I am *not as other men are*, extortioners, unjust, adulterers, or even as this Publican."

His song of praise is not, "God, I thank thee, that, whereas I was once thoughtless, thou hast made me thoughtful—once blind, but thou hast made me see." It is not, "I thank thee that Thou hast made me thus or thus:" but "I thank thee that I am not as the rest of mankind are." He praises *God;* but it is only a thin veil, a poor excuse, for praising *himself*.

How different was the language of St. Paul—"By the grace of God I am what I am." But this man speaks in a boastful spirit—'Others are committing sins; thank God, I am free from them: others are bad; but thank God, I am better than they.' And then, glancing his eye at his fellow-worshipper, he drags him into his prayer, making the sinfulness of the Publican show out *his own* goodness in a more striking manner; just as a dark, dull colour makes a light one appear all the brighter by comparison — "I thank thee, that I am not as this Publican."

Perhaps he was altogether unacquainted with the man: all he knew of him was that he was a Publican. And when he saw him with all the deep earnestness of a penitent, smiting on his breast, and scarcely raising his eyes from the ground, he seems to say, "I am holier than thou. I thank God *I* have no need to beat my breast in that fashion, nor to cast my eyes with shame upon the ground. *I* have done nothing to call for all this."

And then he goes on—"I fast twice in the week. I give tithes of all I possess." All you see is in the same strain of boasting—not one word about his sins—not one petition for grace.

Such was his prayer. And had he then *no* sins to confess? Yes, he had many; but they were hidden. He was like a Sick Man going to the Surgeon, and showing him his sound limbs, but covering up his ulcers.

When we come before God, let us not make the best of ourselves. Let us lay bare all our sores; and ask Him to bind them up, and grant us health and cure.

And now let us take our thoughts off from the Pharisee for a moment, and fix them on the other man—the Publican. He "stands afar off." He has no wish to be seen. He feels that the lowest place in God's House is too good for him. He thinks himself unworthy to come near the Pharisee, who, he takes for granted, must be much holier than himself. He "stands afar off," but not from God; for "the Lord is nigh unto them that are of a broken heart, and saveth such as be of a contrite spirit." Whilst the proud Pharisee is looking upon him with scorn, God is looking upon him with kindness; and the Angels are singing Hallelujahs, that a lost one is found, a sinner restored.

"He would not so much as lift up his eyes to heaven." He seemed to feel like David,

"Mine iniquities have taken hold upon me, so that I am not able to look up." He was ready to exclaim with Ezra, "O my God, I am ashamed and blush to lift up my face to thee." There was a deep and real feeling of humility about him—a feeling of truest self-abhorrence and self-abasement. He felt himself too great a sinner to lift up his eyes to a holy and righteous God. But he did what was far better, he lifted up his heart—that heart which was now softened in repentance, and sighing for relief.

And what was his Prayer? A very short one, but a very earnest one—one that expressed the deep feelings of his soul. There was no attempt to make excuses for himself. He knew his own heart too well, to think that his guilt needed any softening down. His mouth must be stopped: he is guilty before God. There was no comparing himself with his brethren. It was not a time to speak about other men. The matter stood between him and God. Like St. Paul, he felt himself to be "the chief of sinners."

Oh how powerful a man's conviction of sin is, when God really awakens him by His Holy

Spirit. All his false covering is instantly stript off; and he sees himself to be just what he truly is. Then one sin after another is brought to light—sins, that he has long forgotten—sins, that he thought nothing of at the time, and which the world winked at. All these rise up before him; and the weight of them seems like a mountain ready to crush him. He feels as if no other man's sins can be equal to his own.

The Publican's prayer was just the breathing of a soul thus awakened—" God, be merciful to me a sinner." The Pharisee denies himself to be a sinner. None of his neighbours can charge him, and he sees no reason to charge himself, with anything amiss. He is clean; he is pure from sin. But the Publican gives himself no other character than that of a sinner, a convicted criminal at God's bar. He has no dependence, but upon the mercy of God; and *that* he earnestly asks. Mercy, mercy is what he sues for. The Pharisee had spoken of his fasting and his tithe-paying as a merit; but the poor Publican has no idea of any *merit*, but flies to MERCY as his city of refuge.

Has this prayer ever gone up from *your* lips? Or rather I would ask, Has it ever gone up from your heart? Have you ever been humbled in the dust, and felt thoroughly beaten down, because of your sins? Have you ever gone to your Saviour's Cross as a lowly penitent, crying, " God, be merciful to me a sinner"? It may be, you feel that this prayer is just suited to your case.

We have now taken a full view of these two worshippers in the Temple. We have got at something like the state of their hearts—the one proud, boasting, and self-righteous : the other penitent, lowly, and ready to cast himself on the mercy of God. We have examined the prayers, which came from the lips of each. And who would not rather take his place by the side of the meek and humble Publican, little thought of as he was by his fellow-men, than with the proud and scornful Pharisee?

But our Lord, as if to make this beautiful Parable complete, and that it might bring comfort to every broken-hearted penitent, adds, " I tell you, this man went down to his house justified rather than the other." Him, whom the Pharisee would hardly set with the dogs, God sets with the children of His family. His sin is pardoned. His soul is accepted. His prayer, like incense, goes up to heaven, a sacrifice of a sweet savour; whilst the prayer of the other is blown back like smoke: for "God resisteth the proud, but giveth grace to the humble." The one went down from the temple with the same cold dead heart, with which he had gone up: the other with a sweet sense of forgiveness shed abroad in his soul. Thus does God "fill the hungry soul with good things, and the rich he sendeth empty away."

Learn then that God abhors a proud, self-righteous spirit; but He loves to listen to the humble. The Saviour, who has shed His blood for us, is ready to apply that blood to our souls, and to wash out every stain, if only we will acknowledge our guilt, and cling to His cross. He is ready to say to the trembling penitent, "I will: be thou clean." "Though your sins be as scarlet, they shall be white as snow."

Learn too from this Parable that God does not measure our prayers by *the length* of them, or by the *fineness of the words*. Here was a very short prayer, and a very poor one in point of language; but it was an accepted prayer. And if the Lord accepted *such* a prayer from the humble Publican, why not from you or me? Are the words which *he* poured forth unsuited to *our* lips? Have we no sins? Have *we* kept the whole law? If your outward *action* has been correct, have your *thoughts* been always pure? When you look back, far back, into the past, has there been nothing done, which ought to have been left undone— nothing undone, which God has commanded to be done? Like the Pharisee, have *you* no guilt to acknowledge? Is there nothing to be said—nothing but the boastful expression, "God, I thank thee that I am not as other men are"? Will you stand, like him, a guilty creature before your Judge, and boast of your innocence? Will you stand sick and diseased before your Physician, and boast of your health? Will you stand before your merciful Father, ready to forgive, and not ask forgiveness? Have *you* no sins? Oh look into your own heart. Have *you* no need of mercy? Yes, the greatest need.

Oh for more of the spirit of this Publican! We want more of this in our congregations—more of this deep feeling of sin—this heartfelt conviction of our guilt—this smiting on our breasts with godly sorrow—this earnest cry for mercy.

We want more of it in our own souls. Then we shall be, each one of us, hastening to the cross—feeling that only the blood of Christ, only His atonement, can give us relief. We shall long to hear those words of mercy, "Thy sins be forgiven thee; go in peace."

THE TEN VIRGINS.

PART I.

MATT. xxv. 1—5.

"Then shall the kingdom of heaven be likened unto ten virgins, which took their lamps, and went forth to meet the bridegroom. And five of them were wise, and five were foolish. They that were foolish took their lamps, and took no oil with them: but the wise took oil in their vessels with their lamps. While the bridegroom tarried, they all slumbered and slept."

I CAN imagine quite an unlearned man taking up this Parable of the Virgins, and getting from it some precious truth; but at the same time losing much, from not being acquainted with the customs which were observed in the days when it was spoken.

In the country of Judæa, where our Lord dwelt when He was in this world, several customs of the people were altogether different from those in our own land. And we should always bear this in mind, when we read the Word of God.

Now, with regard to the way of conducting marriages in that country some of the ceremonies were entirely unlike anything we have been accustomed to. They usually were performed at night, and in the open air. After the wedding there was generally a Feast, which lasted for three days, and sometimes for as many as seven. It is not certain where this took place—whether in the Bride's house, or in the Bridegroom's. However after a while they proceeded together to their own home, with sounds of music and other signs of rejoicing. The Bride was attended by her Friends and companions; of whom mention is made in the 45th Psalm, "The virgins that be her fellows shall bear her company." But besides these, there was also another party that came out from the house of the Bridegroom, to meet them and welcome them. And these are the Virgins mentioned in the Parable.

And now I hope we shall be better able to understand the Parable before us, or at least that part of it which comes under our notice in the verses before us.

We have here Ten Virgins, who go forth to meet the Bridegroom; to fall in with the procession on its way to the guest-chamber; and to enter with the married pair into their new abode.

The principal Person mentioned here is *the Bridegroom*. And whom is he intended to represent? In one of the other Parables we read of a great King, making a marriage for his Son. The Bridegroom in both cases represents Christ. He is the Bridegroom of His Church. In John iii. He is spoken of by this title. There we find John the Baptist declaring, that he himself was not the Bridegroom, but only the Bridegroom's friend: " I am not the Christ; but I am sent before him. He that hath the bride is the bridegroom; but the friend of the bridegroom, which standeth and heareth him, rejoiceth greatly, because of the bridegroom's voice. This my joy therefore is fulfilled." Again, in Rev. xix, St. John speaks of Christ as the Husband of his Bride. He is describing that glorious time, when our Lord shall come to take to Himself His own people. "I heard as it were the voice of a great multitude, saying, Let us be glad and rejoice, and give honour to him, for the marriage of the Lamb is come, and his wife hath made herself ready. And he saith unto me, Write, Blessed are they which are called unto the marriage supper of the Lamb."

It is very difficult for us to take in at once all that there is in our Lord's blessed character; and therefore He shows Himself to us by little and little, speaking of Himself in ways that we can well understand.

We know, for instance, what a Shepherd is to his sheep; and therefore Jesus calls Himself *our* Shepherd. We know what the Sun is, and what Light is to those who have been sitting in darkness; so Christ calls Himself the Sun and Light of His people. And so too we all know that none are so closely united together as the Husband and the Wife. To show then the nearness of Christ to His people, He is spoken of here as "the Bridegroom." And again Isaiah says, "Thy maker is thy husband."

How thankful we should be for this precious title of our beloved Lord and Saviour. Let us feel great comfort from the thought that He is near us. Let us turn to Him at all times as our refuge. Let us take Him as our Partner through life, and look forward to His companionship for ever. And let us remember that if we do indeed belong to Him —if we are His Bride—then we must be like Him in our hearts and characters. We must love Him above all else. And it must be our delight to hold intercourse with Him, and to be often in His presence.

But we will now turn our attention to those, whom our Parable describes as *going out to meet the Bridegroom*. They are ten in number—ten Virgins. They all *seem* to belong to the Bridegroom's party. They have all *apparently* the same object. And they are each of them carrying in their hands a torch or lamp.

What shall we make of these? It is clear that they are intended to represent Christ's professing people—that large class of persons who are called by His name, who pass for

His followers, and who wish to be counted as "Friends of the Bridegroom." I say, this is a large class. Most of us are *professing* Christians. But when the eye of God rests upon us, He is able to single out numbers who do not *really* belong to Him.

To any one passing by, those Ten Virgins would have seemed much alike. Each had her face turned towards the Bridegroom's house. Each was lifting up the burning lamp. And if a stranger were to come among us, at first sight he would discover but little difference between us. We may go perhaps to the same house of God. We may join in the same prayers. We may sing the same spiritual songs. We may listen to the same sermons. We may even go farther, and draw near to the same Lord's Table. But yet (and oh how affecting the thought) though we now belong to the same Church on earth, we may be, and perhaps shall be, parted in eternity!

Of these Ten Virgins, five were wise, and five were foolish. And there was *this* difference between them—Five of them carried not only a well trimmed, burning lamp, but they also brought with them, each one, a little vessel of spare oil. The others however had merely their lamps; but they had no supply of oil with them.

So it is with ourselves. We all carry the lamp of an outward profession. We go through a round of outward duties. But have we oil in our vessels with our lamps? Have we God's grace? Have we His Holy Spirit dwelling in our hearts?

Ah, be not deceived. You may enjoy great privileges. You may have a fair name among your fellow men. You may have a large amount of head knowledge. And yet you may have no living faith, no warmth of love, no likeness to Christ. How sad it is to think that many a tongue, which has spoken much about heavenly things, shall yet want a drop of water to cool it in " the lake of fire "!

Again, every lamp belonging to these Virgins—all of them—*seemed to burn brightly enough at first.* And so we may make a showy profession of godliness, and men may think that we are really in earnest. But " the Lord knoweth them that are his." We cannot deceive Him. Judas was long looked upon by his brethren as a true disciple. He kept up for some time his profession. But Christ knew his heart all the while. There was no oil there.

In the case of Eliab too we see how little outward appearances are worth. When Jesse brought in his seven sons, for Samuel to choose a king from among them, his eye rested on Eliab the eldest. He had a goodly countenance and a fair look. And Samuel said, "Surely the Lord's anointed is before me." But no. God said, "I have refused him." And then it is added, "For the Lord seeth not as man seeth; for man looketh on the outward appearance, but the Lord looketh on the heart." *We* look upon the mere surface: *His* eye reaches to the inner man. *We* see the lighted lamp, and are satisfied: *He* looks for the oil within.

We are told, in the fifth verse, that "while the bridegroom tarried, they *all* slumbered and slept." This was perhaps natural; for it was now late, and they had been waiting long. Probably nothing is intended by this part of the Parable. And yet such is our conduct in the present day, that we may well take a hint from these words.

Is there not a want of watchfulness and readiness to meet our Lord, even among God's people? That he He *will* come again is a Scripture fact; and we therefore believe it. But do we not feel far too coldly about it? Does it influence our hearts and our lives? Are we indeed like those who are waiting— anxiously waiting—for the coming of their Lord? I verily believe if we were asked, " Had you rather that your Lord should come this day, or this day year"? there would be many, even seriously disposed persons, who would be forced to answer, "I love my Saviour; but I am not prepared—I am not quite ready—for His appearing." Oh how different was the feeling of the Apostle John, who when the Lord declared, " Behold, I come quickly," at once exclaimed with a heart full of love, " Even so come, Lord Jesus."

The early Christians lived in daily expectation of the Saviour's return. He had told them plainly, " Yet a little while and ye shall see me, and again a little while and ye shall not see me, because I go to the Father." "And if I go and prepare a place for you, I will come again, and receive you unto myself; that where I am, there ye may be also."

Now, they believed this. It was to them a living truth. They thought daily and hourly of their returning Lord. They were in a constant state of readiness for His appearing. This was just what He intended. And it is His will that His people should be kept in the same state of preparation from age to age.

It is true, the Bridegroom tarries. Ah, He does so in mercy to our souls. He sees that the fruit is not ripe; the servants are not ready. Had His people been more in earnest, then perhaps He would have gathered them sooner. Yes, He tarries, in mercy. And the Scoffer asks, "Where is the promise of his coming? For since the fathers fell asleep, all things continue as they were from the beginning of creation." So it was in the days of old, when the coming Flood was threatened. "The long suffering of God *waited*, whilst the ark was preparing"; and during those hundred and twenty years, doubtless many a scoffing jest was uttered. Noah's obedience was counted folly; and his preparations groundless. They perhaps said, " He is an alarmist. He is easily frightened. He is taking a gloomy view of things. He is making all these preparations against a day which will never come." The sun shone as brightly in the heavens, and the sky was as cloudless as ever. But God had spoken, and His word came true. Now, "as it was in the days of Noah, so shall it be in the days of the Son of man. They did eat, they drank, they married wives, they were given in marriage, until the day (the very day) that Noah entered into the ark, and the flood came, and it destroyed them all. Even so shall it be in the day when the Son of man is revealed." There will be the very same unbelief, the very same carelessness, the very same lack of preparation.

Let us look to our lamps in time! Yet a little while the Bridegroom tarries. But His tarrying will soon be at an end. He will surely come. Then will every mask be stripped off. Then will every mere professor be discovered. Then it will be clearly seen that "he that hath the Son hath life, and he that hath not the Son of God hath not life."

Oh for something more than a bare profession! Oh for more meetness for the Bridegroom's presence! What we want is more of a watching, waiting, expecting, believing, frame of mind. We want to be numbered among the Bridegroom's real Friends. Then we shall not only be prepared to meet our Lord, but shall "love his appearing." The best news—the most welcome tidings—in our ears will be the cry which shall sound from one end of heaven to the other, "Behold, the Bridegroom cometh; go ye out to meet him"!

THE TEN VIRGINS.

PART II.

MATT. xxv. 6—13.

"And at midnight there was a cry made, Behold, the bridegroom cometh; go ye out to meet him. Then all those virgins arose, and trimmed their lamps. And the foolish said unto the wise, Give us of your oil; for our lamps are gone out. But the wise answered, saying, Not so; lest there be not enough for us and you: but go ye rather to them that sell, and buy for yourselves. And while they went to buy, the bridegroom came; and they that were ready went in with him to the marriage: and the door was shut. Afterward came also the other virgins, saying, Lord, Lord, open to us. But he answered and said, Verily I say unto you, I know you not. Watch therefore, for ye know neither the day nor the hour wherein the Son of man cometh."

THE first part of this Parable has already been explained. We have seen that Christ is represented as the Bridegroom or Husband of His people. We have seen too that the Ten Virgins, who went forth to meet the Bridegroom, are meant to signify all those who profess to be Christ's servants. These were divided into two classes—some wise, and some foolish—some carrying the mere lamp of an outward profession, and some having a supply of oil—that is, the grace of God in their hearts.

The first thing that we notice in the verses before us, is the loud and sudden cry which awakened the Virgins, "Behold, the bridegroom cometh." They had been waiting a long time, and during the Bridegroom's delay, they had fallen asleep. And now, at midnight, a cry is heard along the street where the procession is to pass, "Behold, the bridegroom cometh."

St. Paul speaks of *the suddenness* of our Lord's coming. In writing to the Thessalonians, he says, "Yourselves know perfectly that the day of the Lord so cometh *as a thief in the* night." And I have already called your attention to the sad want of preparation among men—even among Christian men—for that great event.

Look at these Virgins. As soon as the cry awakens them, they turn to their lamps. And this is the first thought that comes across them, "Is my lamp still burning? Is it still alight?" Alas, then it was found that five of the lamps were gone out. The wise had a sufficient supply of oil to keep their lamps burning; but the foolish had none. And how late to make the discovery! The procession was in sight. The Bridegroom was actually coming. And without their lighted lamps they could not join Him. In despair they turn to their companions, saying, "Give us of your oil, for our lamps are gone out."

What discoveries will be made at the day of Christ's appearing! How changed will be the language of many! Those who have thought but little of the Saviour, and despised those who were anxiously waiting for His coming, will then tremble with alarm. Those who have wrapped themselves up, quite satisfied with their own state, will then find out that they have all along been trusting to "a form of godliness" without "the power." Once they thought that all was well with them—that they were rich, and increased with goods, and had need of nothing; but then they will find that much, very much, is wanting. Once they felt angry if their Minister, or some kind Friend, told them that they were wrong. There was a time when they thought that some were too religious, carrying things too far, too thoughtful about their souls. But then they will acknowledge that God's people were in the right—that they were on the safe side —that they were wise for being so much in earnest.

How often a Death-bed brings men to their senses! The world then seems very trifling, and eternity very solemn. Then we feel the nothingness of a mere outward religion, and we long for something better. The empty lamp will not light us. The outward cloke will not cover us. The name of Christian—the mere name—will go for nothing. No, we must have Christ with us, and within us. We must be clothed in His righteousness, and washed in His blood, or we can never sit with Him on His throne.

And now see how vain was the request that these foolish Virgins made to their companions—" Give us of your oil"! It was more than they could give. They had none to spare. All they could hope was that their own lamps might burn bright enough, to allow them to take their part among the bridal company.

There are some things which we *can* give, without making ourselves the poorer. But we cannot give grace. No, this is God's gift; and each one must obtain it for himself. All the advice these wise Virgins could give was, "Go ye rather to them that sell, and buy for yourselves."

Thank God, there is a time when salvation is freely offered to us—offered to the very neediest. There is a time when God says, "Ho, every one that thirsteth, come ye to the waters, and he that hath no money; come ye, buy and eat, without money, and without price."

But there is also a time, when it will be *too*

late to buy. So it was with these Virgins. They were now anxious to procure that which they had so long despised. But the time was gone by. The day of opportunity was past. All was now useless. And we read, "While they went to buy, the Bridegroom came, and they that were ready went in with him to the marriage: and the door was shut."

Think of those words, so full of meaning, "The door was shut." I have already spoken about Noah and the Flood. For a while the door of the ark stood wide open; so that any one, who believed God's word, and trembled at the coming danger, might find a refuge. Noah went about preaching everywhere, and inviting men to come in. The Spirit strove with them. But they only mocked at God's threatenings. At last the day came. Noah entered into the ark; and we read, "The Lord shut him in." How safe, how happy, how secure, was Noah! The rain poured down in torrents. "The fountains of the great deep were broken up." But Noah was under shelter. The very water that was drowning hundreds bore him safely on its bosom.

And now think of those who belonged to the Bridegroom's party in the Marriage Supper-room. The wise Virgins were there; for they were "ready," and went in with him to the marriage. They had now no more need to be anxious about their lamps. Their waiting-time was over. They were with the Bridegroom. And "the door was shut," so that none might now disturb their happiness.

What a picture of that holy and blessed company, who shall be for ever with their Lord in heaven! "They shall hunger no more, neither thirst any more: neither shall the sun light on them, nor any heat; for the Lamb which is in the midst of the throne shall feed them." Their trials will be over—their warfare accomplished—their watchings at an end. They are now safe in their long-looked-for home. "The door is shut," so that no enemy can now disturb them; none can pluck them out of their Saviour's hands. Their language is, "Let us be glad and rejoice, for the marriage of the Lamb is come, and his wife hath made herself ready." " Blessed are they which are called unto the marriage supper of the Lamb."

But alas, whilst we speak of the door being shut as securing for ever the safety of those who are *within*, what shall we say of those who are *without?* Oh, they will cry out in the agony of their hearts, " That door was once open to me, but I would not enter in. There was once written over that door, " OPEN TO EVERY PENITENT"! Now there is written over it, " SHUT FOR EVERMORE."

What will be *our* feeling, if we shall stand at that door hereafter, and find it closed against us? What if we are forced to exclaim in the anguish of our souls, " That door once admitted as great sinners as we are; for they forsook their sins in time, and sought admission. They found a refuge; whilst I am shut out. Manasseh, once so wicked, and David, whose sins were of so deep a dye, were admitted. Saul, once a persecutor, was admitted. The Woman who was a sinner was admitted. Weeping Peter was admitted. The Penitent Thief was admitted. And I, even I, *might* have found admission, but I put mercy from me; and now the door of mercy is for ever closed against me"!

Think of this. And may God enable you to welcome with thankfulness those gracious words of Christ, "I am the Door; by me if any man enter in he shall be saved!"

And now, lest we should miss the great lesson which this Parable is intended to teach us, our Lord bids us in the closing verse, "*Watch* therefore; for ye know neither the day nor the hour wherein the Son of man cometh."

There is great need for the Ministers of Christ to watch both for themselves, and for their people. They are the Lord's "watchmen." They must sound the alarm. They must blow the trumpet, and see that it gives no uncertain sound. They must warn the heedless, and awaken the sleeping.

And those have need to watch who are living careless, thoughtless lives. They have slept too long. Let them beware lest they "sleep the sleep of death."

There is need too for every true servant of

Christ to watch. The world is very enticing. Satan is very busy. Where then does our safety lie? Chiefly I think in prayer. We must be much in prayer, much alone with God.

In these days there is a great deal of activity —a great deal of running to and fro—a great deal of talk about religion. But all this may be, without any heart work—without any watchfulness and preparedness for the great day of our Lord's coming. I am persuaded that one great fault among us is this—we do not spend enough time in retirement, in holding secret communion with our Lord.

This is one great reason why there is not more life and growth among us, and why the work of grace advances so slowly. We know but little of what it is to "enter into our closets," and when we have "shut the door," to speak to "our Father which is in secret." Public Prayer, and the Preaching of the Word are most important means of grace. But if these are allowed to take the place of Private Prayer, and private intercourse with the Saviour, we cannot truly know Him, or be getting ready for His arrival.

You pray, I dare say, morning and evening, and read a portion of God's Word. But I believe a Christian needs something more than this. I believe no Christian can be making rapid strides on the way to heaven, unless he is in the constant habit of retiring for a while from his ordinary business, and putting himself, if it is only for a very few minutes, in the presence of his Lord, and speaking to Him as it were " face to face."

Try this. It will at first seem very difficult. But you will find it most useful. Each day get away for five minutes from your usual occupations, and spend those five minutes in speaking solemnly to Christ, as you would to some one who knows all that is in your heart. This is the way to become acquainted with Him, to realize Him as your Friend, and to look forward to His appearing. This is the way to call down refreshing showers of blessing upon your soul.

I would say to every one who is really anxious to be admitted into heaven, you *must* hold intercourse with God, or your soul will die, your lamp will burn out. You *must* walk with God, or Satan will walk with you. You *must* grow in grace, or you will certainly lose what you have. Be very watchful, or you will not be ready when the Bridegroom cometh. The night is far spent: the day is at hand. The great marriage procession may soon be here. Therefore let us not sleep as do others. Let us wake up before the day dawns. Let us try and be ready. What I say unto you, I say unto all, WATCH!

THE SERVANTS AND THE TALENTS.

MATT. xxv. 14—30.

" For the kingdom of heaven is as a man travelling into a far country, who called his own servants, and delivered unto them his goods. And unto one he gave five talents, to another two, and to another one; to every man according to his several ability; and straightway took his journey. Then he that had received the five talents went and traded with the same, and made them other five talents. And likewise he that had received two he also gained other two. But he that had received one went and digged in the earth, and hid his lord's money. After a long time the lord of those servants cometh, and reckoneth with them. And so he that had received five talents came and brought other five talents, saying, Lord, thou deliveredst unto me five talents: behold, I have gained beside them five talents more. His lord said unto him, Well done, thou good and faithful servant: thou hast been faithful over a few things; I will make thee ruler over many things: enter thou into the joy of thy lord. He also that had received two talents came and said, Lord, thou deliveredst unto me two talents: behold, I have gained two other talents beside them. His lord said unto him, Well done, good and faithful servant: thou hast been faithful over a few things; I will make thee ruler over many things: enter thou into the joy of thy lord. Then he which had received the one talent came and said, Lord, I knew thee that thou art an hard man, reaping where thou hast not sown, and gathering where thou hast not strawed: and I was afraid, and went and hid thy talent in the earth: lo, there thou hast that is thine. His lord answered and said unto him, Thou wicked and slothful servant, thou knewest that I reap where I sowed not, and gather where I have not strawed: thou oughtest therefore to have put my money to the exchangers, and then at my coming I should have received mine own with usury. Take therefore the talent from him, and give it unto him which hath ten talents. For unto every one that hath shall be given, and he shall have abundance: but from him that hath not shall be taken away even that which he hath. And cast ye the unprofitable servant into outer darkness: there shall be weeping and gnashing of teeth."

(See also Luke xix. 11—27.)

THE last Parable which we considered was

the Parable of the Ten Virgins. That pointed to our Lord's coming again; and so does this. That showed how we should *wait* for Him, namely, with our Lamps lighted, and our oil burning: this shows how we should *work* for Him.

A certain great man is here described, as quitting his family for a while, and going "into a far country." He leaves with his servants different sums of money; and after a time he returns, and inquires how each one has discharged his duty.

But you will perhaps say at starting—'It is a thing almost unheard of in these days for a Master to leave with his servants money to be traded with in his absence.' This then requires a word or two of explanation. We are told that servants formerly were often *artisans*, and had money given them to trade with on their Master's account; and were therefore expected to bring him in certain profits. Such were the Servants in the Parable.

These Servants are intended to represent all Christ's professing people. The going into a Far Country represents our Lord going into heaven. And the different Talents committed to the Servants represent the various opportunities which we have of doing good.

And now, in order to understand the Parable fully, and to profit by its teaching, I will break it up into three parts; and examine each separately.

The first part of the Parable seems to show *what our Lord has given us to do for Him during His absence.*

The second part speaks of *the manner in which men ought to fulfil their trust.*

The third part brings before us *the day of reckoning.*

With regard to the first part, which shows how our Lord has employed us during His absence, it appears that He has given to each of us *a special work to do.*

When the man in the Parable sets out for the far country, he calls together his servants, and delivers to them his goods. To one he entrusts goods to the value of five talents, to another two, and to another one. A talent is equal to nearly 400*l*. of our money.

It is very clear from this, that Christ allots to each person a work according to his ability —according to the station which he fills— according to the powers which he possesses. He knows well what we are fitted for, and so He expects from us some return.

But alas, how slow we are to discover this, and act upon it! One man goes to the plough day after day, and labours hard for his bread. Another carefully attends to his family. Another is actively engaged in business. A fourth sits at home, and whiles away his time. But perhaps neither of the four considers that his Lord has placed him here to do *some work for Him*.

I will mention two or three cases. We will begin with *a Minister of Christ*. Is it enough, think you, that he gets through his duties respectably, so that no one can find fault? Is it enough that he keeps on good terms with his flock, and is kind and charitable to those who are in need? Is this all? It is enough perhaps in the world's eyes. They may speak well of him. It would be enough, if only man's approval was wanted. But if he feels as he ought to feel, he will remember that he is entrusted with far more than this; and that more is required of him. He is put in trust with the gospel. He has immortal souls committed to his care. And therefore his one great anxiety—the one thing he labours for, and lives for—should be to save those souls, and serve his heavenly Master.

Or take *a Man of Property*. God has given him wealth, and influence, and leisure. Is it that he may employ these merely to further his own happiness? Has he only to nurse his fortune, to gather around him the comforts of life, and to pass joyously through the world? No, there are talents entrusted to him—great talents, many talents. There is a work to be done for God—something far more important than concerns the mere interests of this present world—a work which bears upon eternity.

Or take *a poor, Labouring man*. He works hard, and pleases his earthly master. He is at his post early in the morning, and comes home late at night. He has not spared himself. But has he done all that is required of him? Truly, his earthly master requires no more. He has served *him* faithfully and well. And yet all the while the great work, which God has given him to do, has perhaps been *altogether neglected.* He may have thought nothing of those important talents, which his absent Lord has committed to his trust. He may have lived utterly in vain, just as if this world was all that concerned him. He may, during a long life, have done no positive good in the world.

We may learn then from this part of the Parable that all—every one of us without exception—have a special work allotted to us by God.

We come now to the second part, which shows us *how we should fulfil our trust.*

Of the Servants in the Parable, two did well. They immediately went and traded with their talents, and made the most of them. And so will every true servant of Christ. He feels that every gift is a talent which he must lay out in his Master's service. He feels it to be a delight and an honour to be employed by Him. He does not ask, "How *little* may I do?" but, "Lord, if thou art pleased to employ me in Thy service, give me grace to labour well and cheerfully for Thee."

It may be said however, "It is true that there are some, who, owing to their stations in life, have clearly many ways of being useful. But how can ordinary people, especially the poor and those who have little influence—how can they either be of use to others, or bring glory to God?

The Servants before us had not an equal amount of goods entrusted to them by their Master. " Unto one he gave five talents, to another two, and to another one: to every man according to his several ability." Observe this expression, "*according to his several ability.*" God measures out His gifts wisely, and He is just as to the return which He requires. We are like so many vessels of different sizes. Every vessel may be full; but some are capable of containing much more than others. God reckons with us according to our ability—according to our capacity. We have *all* something to trade with. Even the lowest and humblest has at all events *one* talent. Yes, we may all be useful. We may all glorify God.

Who is there, for instance, that may not *lead a holy life?* And would not this have its influence on those about us? An ungodly person ruins others besides himself; and a holy person may be the means of saving other souls besides his own. Oh, what a bright and steady light shines forth from one who is really walking with God. Whether he is rich or poor, that man is a blessing in his family, in his village, in his neighbourhood. His words, his ways, his actions, all tell upon those among whom he mixes. Think of this. Your conduct may influence others. Pray to God that His grace may light up your soul, and that you may let your light shine brightly.

Another way, by which you may—any of you—be useful, is by *doing acts of kindness* to those among whom you are thrown. There are ten thousand ways in which a kind Christian spirit may show itself. Thus, whilst the world is cold and selfish, and seems to say,

"Get on as you may—each one for himself" —the Christian may help his Brother, and do much to forward his happiness.

We should lay ourselves out for God, and for one another. We should not grudge a little labour. We should be willing to deny ourselves, if we can by any means be useful. We should often think of our Lord's coming again, when He shall reckon with His servants.

And this brings us at once to the last division of the Parable—*the Master's return—the Day of Reckoning.*

"After a long while," we read, "the lord of those servants cometh, and reckoneth with them." First came the man, who had been intrusted with five talents, and then he who had had two talents. There was no shrinking back with either, for they had both employed well their Master's money. The news of his arrival was joyful news to them; for their conscience told them that all would be well.

And now mark how their Master addresses them, "Well done, good and faithful servant; thou hast been faithful over a few things; I will make thee ruler over many things: enter thou into the joy of thy Lord."

Such will be the cheering language which Christ will address to His faithful and active servants. Oh, how amply He will pay them for all the labour they have spent in His service. And who is there among us that will not then feel, "Oh that I had laboured more for such a Master! Oh that I had been more active in His blessed service!"

But last of all comes the man who had but one talent placed in his hands. His ability, I suppose, was not great; and so but little was intrusted to him. He had only one talent to look after; and yet he neglected to employ it. And miserable indeed was his excuse— "Lord, I know thee, that thou art a hard man, reaping where thou hast not sown, and gathering where thou hast not strawed; and I was afraid, and went and hid thy talent in the earth. Lo, there thou hast that is thine." In answer to this, the Master seems to say, "I will meet you on your own ground. Supposing that this hard character you have given me was all true. Supposing that I was all you say—that I was one who reaps where I sowed not, and gathers where I have not strawed. Supposing I was a hard taskmaster, like Pharaoh, requiring the bricks, but refusing the straw—even upon this shewing, you are without excuse."

But was this the real character of the lord in the Parable? And is this the character of our Master in heaven? It *is* the character which ungodly men are apt to give Him. In their wicked hearts they think Him even such an one as themselves. They do not believe in His forgiving love, and His willingness to accept their work with all its faults, provided it is done with a true heart, and with an honest desire to please Him.

The slothful and wicked servant will be utterly without excuse. God will punish such an one both here, and in the world to come. As regards his present punishment, the Lord will say, " Take his talent from him, and give it to him that hath ten talents." And then, in the world to come, his punishment will be completed, " Cast ye the unprofitable servant into outer darkness: there shall be weeping and gnashing of teeth."

Now, just observe what was this man's

crime. He had not wasted his Master's goods, like the Unjust Steward. He had not spent all his portion in riotous living, like the Prodigal. Nor was he ten thousand talents in debt, like the Unmerciful Servant. No, he had not been actually dishonest. But he had hid his lord's money in the earth. He had neglected to make the best use of it. He was an *unprofitable* servant.

Do not suppose then, because you have done no great harm—because you have not been guilty of any great crime—*therefore* God will acquit you. There are many who say to themselves, " I have never injured my neighbour. I have never despised God's Ministers, or ridiculed His Bible. I have never taken His name in vain. I have never wasted His gifts in drunkenness or gluttony." This may be; but for all that, you may still be sadly wanting. You may have been a barren tree in the vineyard, a withered member in the Christian body, a drone in the hive. And your portion may be to be " cast into outer darkness, where there is weeping and gnashing of teeth."

Do not excuse yourself by saying, " So little

has been committed to my charge, that it matters not how I employ it. At the best I cannot do much for God's glory. What signifies the little, whether it be done, or left undone?" Now, this Parable shews us that the Lord looks for faithfulness in *little*, as well as in *much*, and will deal with us accordingly.

And now let the consideration of this Parable convince us that we are "not our own, but are bought with a price," and therefore we should endeavour to "glorify God in our bodies, and in our spirits, which are his."
And do not stop there. Ask yourself, *How* may I be useful? *How* can I carry out the advice here given me? *What* can I do to glorify God? *How* can I act so as to please Him? Let this be our great desire; and then, when our Lord returns, we shall be numbered among His good and faithful servants, and enter into His joy for ever.

And now I have finished my examination of our Lord's Parables. It has indeed been an interesting task to me, and I trust not less so to you. God grant that He, from whose lips they came, may have spoken by them to our hearts, and taught us to understand better, and to feel more love for, His Truth!

Perhaps at some future time, when you are reading one of these Parables, some word which has been written here may come back to your mind, and bring comfort to your soul. I believe that the closer we look into these "earthly stories with a heavenly meaning," spoken by our Lord Himself, the more inclined we shall be to exclaim, "Never man spake like this man;" "Who teacheth like him?"

LONDON: WILLIAM MACINTOSH, 24, Paternoster-row.

www.ingramcontent.com/pod-product-compliance
Lightning Source LLC
Chambersburg PA
CBHW030321240426
43673CB00040B/1234